LOOKING AT GOD'S APPOINTMENT CALENDAR

Bringing People Together-
Stories Past, Present and Future

CARL M. MCCONCHIE

WESTBOW
PRESS®
A DIVISION OF THOMAS NELSON
& ZONDERVAN

WestBow Press books may be ordered through booksellers or by contacting:

WestBow Press
A Division of Thomas Nelson & Zondervan
1663 Liberty Drive
Bloomington, IN 47403
www.westbowpress.com
844-714-3454

ISBN: 979-8-3850-0366-2 (sc)
ISBN: 979-8-3850-0367-9 (e)

Library of Congress Control Number: 2023914410

Print information available on the last page.

WestBow Press rev. date: 08/22/2023

I dedicate this writing to the people of North Leverett Baptist Church who allowed me to be their pastor for almost thirty-one years and who made it possible for me to undertake nine mission trips to Minsk, Belarus over a period of eleven years.

AKNOWLEDGEMENTS

I am very grateful for the several people who have contributed to this writing, either by extensive proof reading, or reading it for the purpose of content evaluation and encouragement. Thank you: Pam Williams, Sally Imhoff, Pastor Robert McIntyre, Richard Kuehmichel, Sandy Samaniego, Don and Sara Robinson and of course, my wonderful wife of many years, Phyllis.

CONTENTS

SECTION ONE—APPOINTMENTS PAST AND PRESENT

SECTION TWO—APPOINTMENTS FUTURE

APPENDIX SECTION

SECTION ONE

APPOINTMENTS
PAST AND PRESENT

THE HINDU SCIENTIST

SOMEWHERE OVER THE NORTH ATLANTIC

"Can you tell me what is in the Bible? I don't know anything about the Bible," she said. That was the request that was directed to me on my trip across the Atlantic between Europe and Boston, the shortest I could have ever imagined, as to my sense of it. After that question was presented to me, a movie came on the screens of that Boeing-747. When the movie was over and the screens went dark, we were still talking. We spoke about the Bible and the Gospel of Christ for hours.

After boarding the plane in Frankfurt, Germany, I took my seat on the left side of the plane where there was a row of two seats. I always requested the aisle seat when I traveled to give me freedom of movement during the long trips. Lufthansa always granted my request. After a while, a young woman approached. She had the window seat next to mine. She was not very tall, so I assisted her in getting her carry-on up to the over-head compartment. I told her to please feel free to ask me to move anytime she wanted to get out into the aisle. She smiled. At that point I wondered as to her nationality. It was not until much later that she told me she was Hindu. She was from India.

This was my last trip of nine that I made to Minsk, Belarus, to teach in a Bible College there. Each trip took about three weeks, including travel time, to teach one course of theology. I spent about 50 hours with the students each time. A Christian organization, now known as "Cru" recruited American pastors for these short- term mission trips. The school there, the Evangelical Bible College of Belarus, recruited the students. When Lee Harvey Oswald, the man who shot president Kennedy, defected to the Soviet Union, he lived in the city of Minsk and married a Russian speaking woman. I saw the house where he lived while there, as it was pointed out to me.

This was to be my final trip. Each time I was over there I sensed a special presence and enablement of the Spirit of God. Almost every time I was there, I met and came to know someone who was not a part of the school. In addition to the students at the school I met other people with whom I could share the Scripture. At this point I would like to share the fact that by nature I am not an extrovert. I have always been a little on the shy side. As I have grown older, I am more and more less so. I could always speak on subjects in a class or from the pulpit, but I was not good at initiating conversation with strangers. That's what makes these encounters the more amazing. Concerning my trips to Belarus, I would come home each time to my church and relate some unusual experience I had had on my trip. Prior to this trip I was leading singing at a Men's Retreat when in response to the sharing of my special encounters with people, one man said to me, "You will meet someone on this trip also." Well, I looked for such a person while I was there in Minsk on my next trip, but this time I met no one, that is until I met the woman on the plane.

We said nothing to each other for a good while. She was reading a book and I noticed that it was "The Da Vince Code." I said "How do you like the book?" "Oh," she said, "it's interesting." She then left her seat to go to the facility. I then took that opportunity to go to the overhead compartment to retrieve my briefcase. I wanted to get a U.S News and World Report magazine that I had purchased at the airport in Boston at the beginning of my trip. In it was a several page article on the Da Vince Code. In those days the matter was very much in the news. I also wanted to get from my briefcase a pictorial church directory that showed my church and revealed what I did there as its pastor. When she came back, I showed her the magazine article and she was very interested. Then I showed her the church directory and she was amazed to learn what my occupation was.

She had told me earlier that she was returning from a conference in Madrid. She was involved in scientific research as a graduate student at the University of Massachusetts in Amherst, Ma. She was involved in research in the field of DNA. Now at this point I was astounded. As a student she was living perhaps ten miles from where I lived in Massachusetts. I began to wonder if this was something that the Lord had especially arranged.

I do not remember exactly how it began, but I pointed out some of the historical errors in the Da Vinci Code. She said, "How can they write that?" She was believing what I was telling her. It was soon after in our conversation that she asked the question; "I don't know anything about the Bible. Would you tell me what is in the Bible?" She said, "My friends tell me that I shouldn't be interested in spiritual things because I'm a scientist. But I am." This led to our long conversation about what was in the Bible. I was saying to myself, "This is extraordinary, this is amazing. Here I am many miles from home, sharing Christ with a Hindu who is also many miles from home, but who lives next door to me, so to speak. The Lord has set this up. He has brought us together." It occurred to me that this was on His appointment calendar. She was seeking God before she ever sat down beside me.

We kept talking. All too soon we had to leave the airplane. We exchanged names and phone numbers. As we prepared to go through customs at Logan airport it became evident that we would be in two different lines, one for American citizens and the other for non-citizens. She called to me from her line and said, "I will call you." She was indeed interested in more conversation. But I also knew that her husband was meeting her at the airport. He would likely not approve of her getting advice from a Christian. She did not call. But later I called and learned that she was doing her research at that time in Boston. I encouraged her to continue her search in the area of spiritual things. Very often since then I have prayed for Illa; that is her name. I truly expect to see her in God's presence someday. As I have become older, I am looking forward to seeing people there. Everyone I have ever known who were believers, I will see there. I will remember every name. There will be no language barriers, such as I encountered in Minsk and elsewhere. I look forward to renewing my conversation with the Hindu scientist that I met on the plane. Nevertheless, for me to have a seat next to a Hindu woman on a trans-Atlantic flight and have her ask me to tell her what was in the Bible, that was to my heart and mind beyond amazing. I know that the events of that day had been written on God's appointment calendar.

I relate the above story by way of instruction because this is a book about God -ordained appointments, often times very remarkable as to the details of His working.

INTRODUCTION TO
SECTION ONE — PART TWO

In the book of Acts there are three people that have one special thing in common. Yes, they are all Gentiles. But in addition to that we find in each case that they are moving toward God before a servant of God is sent to them.

Philip is sent to meet with an Ethiopian eunuch as recorded in Acts 8. But the story there reveals that this man has already gone to great lengths to satisfy his heart with a knowledge of the true God. Peter is sent to meet Cornelius, a Roman centurion. We read that he is **"...a devout man who feared God with all his household, and gave many alms to the Jewish people and prayed to God continually (Acts 10:2)."** Then we read in verse 4 of Acts 10, **"What is it Lord? And he said to him, 'Your prayers and alms have ascended as a memorial before God.'"** Paul is sent to Lydia, a business-woman from Thyatira, a seller of purple fabrics. We read in Acts 16:14 that she **was "worshiper of God."** At Philippi she met Paul by a riverside there. She was listening to his teaching when **"the Lord opened her heart to respond to the things spoken by Paul** (Acts 16:14)."

We intend to get into and explore these remarkable stories found in the book of Acts. Pastor John MacArthur makes this statement in his commentary on Acts, "That God rewards the seeking heart is the clear teaching of Scripture. In Jeremiah 29:13 God said, '**You will seek Me and find Me, when you search for Me with all your heart,**' while in John 7:17 the Lord Jesus Christ said, '**If any man is willing to do His will, he shall know of the teaching, whether it is of God, or whether I speak from Myself.**'" [John MacArthur p. 254]

(See end notes for information on authors]). It is my firm belief that when a man or woman begins to send up positive signals to Him, He responds by sending someone or provides some means by which the message of the gospel is given so as to enable saving faith to salvation. And very often, as seen in Acts chapters 8,10 and 16, God sets up a divine appointment so as to bring together His servant and the one who is seeking.

We bear in mind also that Jesus said in John 6:44, **"No one can come to Me, unless the Father who sent Me draws him: ..."** We also read in John 6:36, **"All that the Father gives me will come to Me, and the one who come to Me, I will certainly not cast out."** This is in the context of the statement that many of the people who were following Him were not really believing in Him. We will rather focus on the words of Jesus found in John 7:17, **"...if any man is willing to do His will...,"** noting the fact the Holy Spirit is very much in view in this whole section of scripture. The three people mentioned here are drawn to Him and are seeking Him before God sends someone to meet with them. [See Appendix for a brief essay on Election versus Free Will.]

If the reader will bear with me, I will include two or three stories of divine appointment that I have experienced. Dear reader, it could happen to you. The Lord might unexpectedly bring someone across your path that is ready to receive the message of salvation. God sets up the appointment. Of course, the Holy Spirit works in it all. He draws men and women to Himself and provides the light that brings them to Jesus Christ. The Holy Spirit is very prominent in these chapters of the book of Acts. Again, we bear in mind that it is God who put's these people on His appointment calendar.

CHAPTER ONE

PHILIP AND THE PRINCE

THE ETHIOPIAN

"He was a man of great authority." Those words are found in the American Standard Version of 1901 as it translates Acts 8:27. Those words are also found in the King James Version, as well as the New King James Version. "**'Of great authority**" is all one word in Greek, *dynastes,* from which we get the word 'dynasty.' It is translated "**the mighty**" in Luke 1:52 (KJV and RSV). Elsewhere in the New Testament it occurs only in I Timothy 6:15, where God is called '**Potentate.**' The word means 'prince, ruler, potentate'." [Charles W. Carter and Ralph Earle, p.118.]

So, the Ethiopian eunuch, that we read of in Acts 8:27, is more than just an important man or high official in the court of Queen Candace. He is something of a prince. We don't mean of course that he had royal blood in his veins, but that as the overseer of the Queen's treasure he was a very powerful man. He was a *dynastes*, as noted above, a term even used of

God Himself. He may or may not have been a eunuch in the literal sense. I have read several sources which point out that although the term originally had reference to the servants who looked after the king's harem, who were indeed emasculated men, the term came to be used of other officials who served the king or queen. (I discovered that in the Encyclopedia Britannica some years ago.) It is interesting that in Genesis 39:1 we read, "**Now Joseph had been taken down to Egypt; and Potiphar, an Egyptian officer of Pharaoh, the captain of the body-guard bought him from the Ishmaelites, who had taken him down there.**" The word used there of Potiphar in the Hebrew and in the Greek translation of the Old Testament (the Septuagint) is "eunuch." But later we find in the story that Potiphar was married. I have also noticed that terminology used in Daniel chapter one of the officials who looked after Daniel. We don't see it in the English translations but in Hebrew it's the word for eunuch. If this Ethiopian was literally a eunuch, he would have been denied access to the temple, according to Deut. 23:1. He therefore would have been "unable to participate fully in the Jewish worship services" (MacArthur, p. 254). Some commentators believe that he was a eunuch in the literal sense. If so, the words of Isaiah would have been a great encouragement to him. "**For thus says the Lord to the eunuch who keep My Sabbaths, and choose what pleases Me, and hold fast my covenant, to them I will give in My house and within My walls a memorial, and a name better than that of my sons and daughters; I will give them an**

2

everlasting name which will not be cut off (Isaiah 56:4,5)." Perhaps that is why he was drawn to the book of Isaiah.

THE MAN OF GOD

Philip was one of the seven, as recorded in Acts chapter 6, who were selected to assist the work of the Apostles. They were to be "...**men of good reputation, full of the Spirit and of wisdom, whom we may put in charge of this task** (Acts 6:3)." This is in the context of a dispute between the Hellenistic *Jews* (Jews born in other countries) and the Native *Jews,* because their widows were being overlooked in the daily serving of food. This was not just a matter of helping to serve tables. It involved dealing with people and their issues. There was an ongoing dispute and, therefore, a need for the wisdom of a Spirit filled man. Philip was such a man. Stephen was also such a man, and his great work, testimony and martyrdom are recorded in chapters 6-8 of the book of Acts.

THE SUCCESSFUL EVANGELIST

Beginning in verse 4 of Acts chapter 8 we read of the great work of evangelism that was taking place in Samaria. "**Philip went down to the city of Samaria and *began* proclaiming Christ to them** (Acts 8:5)." His great success was stated in verse 6 of Acts chapter 8, "**The crowds with one accord were giving attention to what was said by Philip, as they heard and saw** the signs which he was performing." And then we read in verse 8 of Acts chapter 8. **"So, there was much rejoicing in that city."** His heart, also, must have been filled with great joy and a sense of fulfillment in what the Lord was doing in his life.

A CHANGE OF MISSION

Unexpectedly, we can assume, **an angel of the Lord spoke to him** and said, **"...go south to the road that descends from Jerusalem to Gaza. (This is a desert road) (Acts 8:26)."** So now, from Samaria and passing down through Jerusalem, traveling about 50 miles down to what we now call the Gaza Strip, he leaves his ministry to the multitudes and finds himself in the middle of nowhere, as we might say, to keep an appointment with one man. That man is to become, perhaps, the first African convert. According to verse 27 of Acts chapter 8 there is now no hesitation, **"So he got up and went;"**

BEHOLD

The very next word in the Greek text is one which some of the new translations, including the one that I prefer, exclude. It is the word **"behold (Acts 8:27)."** According to Greek scholar and commentator J.A. Alexander, "Behold, as usual denotes something unexpected." [J.A. Alexander, p.341.] It was a strange mission, indeed, but what Philip now sees is very much unexpected. It must have astounded him to see, here in the desert, this scene. It is not a picture of a man traveling alone, as J. Vernon McGee points out; "He had a great retinue of servants and minor officials with him. He wasn't sitting in a chariot with the reins in one hand and a book in the other as we see sometimes see him pictured. This man was sitting back in a chariot, protected from the sun by a canopy. He had a private chauffeur and was riding in style." [J. Vernon McGee, p. 100]

HE WAS A SEEKER

He is called an Ethiopian, but that term used here does not correspond with modern-day Ethiopia. The reference is to a land on the Nile located south of Egypt. It was rather Nubia which is largely today's Sudan. As far as the Greeks and Romans were concerned, Nubia was very far away. It was far south. We might say it was the "outer limits." This man, who is referred to as an Ethiopian, therefore had traveled a long way so as to satisfy his heart's longing to know the true God. He had traveled all the way from Nubia, south of Egypt to Jerusalem and is now on his way back. We read here that he was reading from Isaiah. He had perhaps paid a great deal of money for that scroll. We can imagine that the Jewish leaders there did not give them away freely. How had he come to know about Judaism? According to John MacArthur there was a large Jewish colony in Alexandria [MacArthur, p. 254]. Had he become a proselyte? If so, he would have been circumcised and would have endeavored to keep all the laws of the Judaism of the day. (As mentioned before, if he was literally a eunuch, he might not have been permitted to do that.) But if he just came to the Jewish synagogues and listened to the scriptures, he would have been called a "**God Fearer**." [New King James Study Bible p. 1724]. But what is presented before us in Acts chapter 8 is a classic case of one who is seeking to know God. And that is what this book is about, people who are seeking after God and who are given an appointment with a servant of God.

As is always the case, the Holy Spirit used the Word of God to draw people to Himself. We find here that the eunuch was reading from Isaiah, chapter 53:32,33, "**He was led as a sheep to slaughter; and as a lamb before it's shearer is silent, so He does not open His mouth. In humiliation His judgment was taken away; who will relate this generation? For His life was removed from the earth.**"

In a magazine entitled, "Israel My Glory" there is a section that appears in every edition of the magazine. It is called, "Apples of Gold." I always turn to that section when the magazine arrives. It is the testimony of a man whose name is Zvi Kalisher. (He has since passed away). He had lived in Jerusalem and in each edition of that magazine, he tells of his efforts to reach the Rabbis and Orthodox Jews there. In doing so he almost always calls their attention to Isaiah 53. In one session he asks them, "Why do you boycott the words of God that are written in the Bible?" "We have never boycotted even one letter from the Bible," one said. Zvi replied, "Not just one letter. You boycott a whole chapter…The fact is you boycott Isaiah 53. Why are you so afraid of that chapter?" In almost every story that Zvi Kalisher shares with us, he tells of pointing the Jews today to Isaiah 53. [My Glory magazine, p. 42.] To avoid the true meaning of the passage, it is common today for Jewish scholars to say that the "Suffering Servant" of Isaiah is a reference to Israel itself.

HIS QUESTION

The Holy Spirit tells Philip to "**go up and join this chariot** (Acts 8:29)." Perhaps it was an ox cart and thus moving very slowly. Oxen are known to have a great deal of endurance when traveling long distances and would have been suitable for such a journey. The cart or wagon moving slowly, Philip would have no trouble catching up to it. And Philip says, "**Do you understand what you are reading** (Acts 8:30)?" The Eunuch says, "**How could I unless someone guides me?** (Acts 30-31)." In other words, "Can you tell me what it means?" That is the question that opens up that which was, perhaps, a long session of sharing the meaning of scripture with this man.

"**Look! Water! What prevents me from** being **baptized** (Acts 8:36)?" His heart was ready. He didn't want to wait any longer. Somewhere along the way he had come to believe in Jesus as his Savior. In their long talk Philip had apparently told the Eunuch about the importance of being baptized. And it just so happened, I speak facetiously, water was provided at that moment. Rather, it was all in accordance with God's sovereign plan. In the desert they just happened to come to water at that moment. We read that they both "**went down into the water**" (Acts 8:38) and they both "**came up out of the water.**" It wasn't just a small puddle or a trickle of water (Acts 8:39).

Verse 37, of Acts chapter 8, is not found in the earliest and thus better manuscripts. It reads, "**If you believe with all your heart, you may.**" And he answered and said, "**I believe that Jesus is the Son of God.**" The New American Version puts it in brackets, while the NIV and ESV simply omit it. It would be convenient to have it there since it shows that saving faith must come before baptism. However, we might assume that Philip communicated to the man at some point what the verse suggests.

Then we read, "**When they came up out of the water, the Spirit of the Lord snatched Philip away and the eunuch no longer saw him** (Acts 8:39)" The question is: Do we have here a miracle? The NASB says, "**snatched away.**" Another version might read, translating Acts 8:39, "**took away.**" Or a translation could say "**carried away.**" Do we have here a miracle? Some commentators say that is not necessary to see here a miraculous rapture. But I can see it, possibly, as a miraculous sign to this Ethiopian. We bear in mind that this takes place in the Apostolic age when signs were granted in order to authenticate the work of the Apostles and others. Philip himself had performed signs (Acts 8:6).

WHO DOES THE FOLLOW UP?

In the work of evangelism, we often stress that follow up is very important when people came to faith in Christ. Here we read that the Ethiopian "**no longer saw him** (Acts 8:39)." Wow! What's to become of this new babe in Christ? Does it suggest in the text here that Phillip somehow just vanished? It says "**he no longer saw him** (Acts 8:39)." That would support the thought that a miracle occurred here. That would make this encounter very real to this man. He is not about to forget the whole supernatural nature of the meeting with Philip if God's servant is suddenly snatched away.

But as to the question of "follow up", we note that the Holy Spirit is presented as being very active in the book of Acts. I think that when someone comes to Christ and there is no opportunity for follow-up, we must commit the individual to the care of the Holy Spirit. If the Holy Spirit has led someone to Christ and provided the means for his coming to faith, He will somehow, by some means, take care of the new believer. We read in Ephesians 4:30 that the believer is "**sealed by the Spirit unto the day of redemption**" If his faith is genuine and he has been born again, the Holy Spirit will work in his life and protect him unto "**the day of redemption**." We have been redeemed by the precious blood of Christ.

To sum up, we can say of the Ethiopian that he is a classic case of a "seeker." He went to great lengths to fill the void in his heart that only God could fill.

We conclude this chapter with a final word from Vernon McGee: "Philip is snatched off the page of Scripture. He is not needed here anymore. The Ethiopian rides off the pages of Scripture in his chariot. He went on his way rejoicing." Now what about this man? Vernon McGee writes, "The first great church was not in the United States, nor was it in Europe, nor was it in Jerusalem, nor was it in Asia Minor. The first great church was in northern Africa. The Ethiopian evidently went back and through his witness and his influence, a church was begun there [Vernon McGee, page 103]." Perhaps so.

John MacArthur has this to add, "According to the church father, Irenaeus, he became a missionary to the Ethiopians," quoting Rickard N. Longnecker, [p.386]. "But the genuine records of the Ethiopian church go back only as far as the fourth century [Carter and Earle, p.121]." "What is clear is that the Spirit's preparation coupled with Philip's presentation, produced in him the faith that does save" [MacArthur, p.260].

CHAPTER TWO

THE ROMAN COMMANDER

The Greek word is "hekatontarches." It means "ruler of a hundred." The word occurs twenty-one times in the New Testament. It is translated "centurion." **"Now there was a man at Caesarea named Cornelius, a centurion of what was called the Italian cohort (Acts 10:1)."** Usually, a centurion was the commander of one hundred men, but I have read in several commentaries on this verse written by Greek scholars that in this case he might have commanded a much greater number. J.A. Alexander, F.F. Bruce, Charles W. Carter and Ralph Earle, in their commentaries on Acts, point out that in some cases, especially in remote areas of the Roman world, there is given latitude to the term. He could have commanded a subdivision of the legion. The word "band" in verse 1 of Acts 10 probably means such a subdivision. J. A. Alexander in his commentary on Acts, [Page 388)] believes that the word "cohort" here should be translated "band." And the word "band" here would refer to such a subdivision of the legion. Carter and Earle suggest that he could have been the commander of six hundred men

[Carter and Earle, p. 137]. The reference to the Italian band means that they were recruited in Rome.

F.F. Bruce quotes the Roman historian, Polybius, "'Centurions were the backbone of the Roman army. ...They are required not to be bold and adventurous so much as good leaders, of steady and prudent mind, not prone to take the offensive or start fighting wantonly, but able when overwhelmed and hard-pressed to stand fast and die at their post. [Bruce p.215]'" It is interesting that "the centurions who make their appearance in the NT record all make a favorable impression. It is to be noted that the first Gentile with whom Jesus had dealings in His public ministry (so far as we are informed) was a Roman Centurion, and that it was with reference to this man's faith that He said, 'many shall come from the east and the west, and shall sit down with Abraham, and Isaac and Jacob, in the kingdom of heaven (Matt. 8:11).' These words now begin to find their fulfillment in another centurion." [Bruce, p. 215] This man, indeed, was an influential, powerful and, perhaps, wealthy man.

A PROSELYTE OF THE GATE

That term was used to refer to "a God fearer" as opposed to one who was actually a proselyte to the Jewish faith. We gather from the words here that he, Cornelius, was probably not circumcised, nor was he one who observed all the precepts of the law of Moses (dietary, sabbaths, etc.). But he was "**a devout**

man and one who feared God with all his household, and gave many alms to the _Jewish_ people and prayed to God continually (Acts 10:2)." The word _Jewish_ is not in the Greek text, but is implied in the whole context. He seems to have loved the Jewish people and the Jewish God. He probably attended the synagogue services and listened to the word of God.

We note here the words of God directed to the father of the nation Israel, as found in Genesis 12: **"And I will make you a great nation, And I will bless you, and make your name great, and I will bless those who bless you, And the one who curses you I will curse, and in you all the families of the earth will be blessed (Genesis 12:2-3)."** Cornelius was certainly a man who blessed Israel. Many have not and I think they will regret it when they stand before God someday. In verse 1 of chapter 10 of Acts we read of a man who was about to realize that God has arranged for him an appointment with His foremost apostle at the time, Peter. Cornelius had been sending up positive signals (as someone has put it) to the one true God. He had been responding to the light that he had and God was now going to give him all the light that he needed.

We are impressed also that Cornelius was not only a godly man in his private worship, but his influence extended to his whole household. This seems to include family members, servants, and soldiers. We read in verse 7 of Acts chapter 10 that, **"...he summoned two of his servants and a devout soldier of those who were his personal attendants."** Later when Peter arrived and delivered his message to them, they were all gathered and ready to listened to him and not only that, they all responded to the message while he was still speaking. "**While Peter was still speaking these words, the Holy Spirit fell upon all those who were listening to the message (Acts 10:44).**" And then we read in verses 47 and 48 of Acts chapter 10 that they were baptized in water. Not only had Cornelius been sending up those positive signals, but his influence was such that his whole household was seeking after God. "Positive signals" is terminology that I borrowed from a man who came to speak at our seminary chapel at Dallas Seminary, back around 1960. His name, as I recall, was Robert Thieme. He spoke of "positive signals" and "negative signals.") In Romans chapter 1 we have the negative signals that men have sent up. They have turned away from the knowledge of God that can be seen in creation (Romans 1:18-20). Therefore, Paul writes in Romans 1:20, "...**they are without excuse**." This book is about people who have responded to the light that God has given them and have sent up "positive signals." Cornelius is clearly such a person.

Let's come back to verse 30 where Cornelius recounts what the angel of the Lord said to him, **"Four days ago to this hour, I was praying in my house during the ninth hour; and behold, a man stood before me in shining garments, and he said, 'Cornelius, your prayer has been heard and your alms have been remembered before God (Acts 10:31,32).'"** Back in verse 4 of Acts chapter ten we read that the angel said to him, "...**Your prayers and alms**

have ascended as a memorial before God (Acts 10:4)."
Carter and Earle state that the Greek word for "memorial"
was "used in the Septuagint (an ancient Greek version of
the Old Testament) to translate the Hebrew word which is
a name given to that portion of the vegetable oblation [meat
offering, KJV] which was burnt with frankincense upon
the altar, the sweet savor, of which ascending to heaven,
was supposed to commend the person sacrificing to the
remembrance and favor of God [Carter and Earle, p.137]."
In the words of that old hymn, "Sweet Hour of Prayer," the
prayer time of Cornelius was not only sweet to him, but also
to God. I wonder if his knowledge of Judaism allowed him
to understand what the angel meant by "memorial." But
Cornelius has clearly been sending up those positive signals.
This book is about people who have responded to the light
that God has given them and have sent up "positive signals".
Cornelius is clearly such a man.

IT'S EXPLICIT

This appointment is clearly laid out. In response to his
prayers, an angel comes to him. He is told to send to Joppa for
the man that he is to meet. Peter is told to go north to Caesarea
to meet with a man named Cornelius. It's all laid out in a long
and significant narrative.

I have suggested that we might have divinely planned
appointments. But it very may often be implicit. We say, "I think

God has brought me to this person." We take it by faith. We think, "this is so remarkable that God must have arranged it." But in the book of Acts, it's all laid out because very important matters are taking place in the early church, matters important to good Christian doctrine. This is an extended passage of scripture concerning the gospel going out to the Gentiles and the need for the believing Jews to understand that fact.

HE SPOKE IN TONGUES

So far, we have been impressed with the greatness of this man as well as his devotion to the one true God. But now we read that he spoke in "tongues." **"For they were hearing them speaking in tongues and exalting God ... (Acts 10:46)."** Not only Cornelius, but apparently his entire household, who readily responded to the preaching of Peter, began to speak in tongues when the Holy Spirit fell upon them. We read in verse 44 of Acts chapter 10, **"While Peter was still speaking these words, the Holy Spirit fell upon all those who were listening to the message."** How strange it is that we find this Roman commander, this devout man, suddenly experiencing this gift of the Spirit! To appreciate this event, we must understand God's plan for the spreading of the Gospel and the building up of the Church of Christ as laid out in the book of Acts.

THE PROMISE OF THE SPIRIT

Let us now scan the first eleven chapters of the book of Acts noting, first of all, three key verses found in chapter one:

"Gathering them together, He commanded them not to leave Jerusalem, but to wait for what the Father had promised, 'Which,' *He said*, 'you heard from Me; for John baptized with water, but you will be baptized with the Holy Spirit not many days from now (Acts 1:4-5).'" **"...but you will receive power when the Holy Spirit has come upon you; and you will be my witnesses both in Jerusalem, and in all Judea and Samaria, and even to the remotest part of the earth (Acts 1:8)."**

The first ones to receive the gift of the Spirit were Jews; some are Jews who were living in Palestine and some who were Hellenistic Jews, those from other countries who had come back to Jerusalem for the observance of Pentecost. We assume that the promise of the Spirit is first realized at Pentecost as described in Acts chapter 2. Those who were enabled to receive the Spirit and spoke in tongues were Jews and the phenomenon was readily observed by all present.

Finally, the general outline of Acts having been presented in Acts 1:8, we now move on to Samaria. We find in chapter 8, as noted before, Philip is having a great deal of success as he proclaims Christ in Samaria and so we read, beginning in verse 14 of Acts chapter 8:

> **"Now when the apostles in Jerusalem heard that Samaria had received the word of God, they sent them Peter and John, who came and prayed for them that they might receive the Holy Spirit. For He had not yet fallen upon any of them; they had simply been baptized in the name of the Lord Jesus. They began laying hands on them, and they were receiving the Holy Spirit (Acts 8:14-17)."**

It is not stated in this passage that the Samaritan believers were enabled to speak in *tongues*. We can assume that and I think they did. We can safely assume that these Samaritans, who were genetically part Jewish and part Gentile, are the second group established within the body of Christ. They are the second people-group to receive the Baptism of The Spirit.

Now we come back to the all-important story of Cornelius, the Roman Centurion. In Acts chapter10 we read of a vision, that Peter saw, of a great sheet being lowered down from heaven, in which there were all kinds of animals, clean and unclean (Acts 10:10-17). Peter is commanded to eat even that, which under the law, was deemed unclean. The great lesson, of course, is that the Gospel is to be preached to the Gentiles, who had been regarded as unclean.

THE BIG QUESTION

How do we convince the Jewish believers that Gentiles should be welcomed into the Body of Christ, the Church? Are they to simply take Peter at his word? "Perhaps he was confused," they might think, as to what he really saw or dreamed. Are we supposed to believe that Gentile believers are to be received into our body of believers? It is important to take note of the following verses found in Acts chapter 11 where Peter is reporting back to Jerusalem as to what had happened in Caesarea with Cornelius and the Gentiles there:

> **"And I remembered the word of the Lord, how He used to say, 'John baptized with water, but you will be baptized with the Holy Spirit.' Therefore, if God gave to them the same gift as *He* gave us also after believing in the Lord Jesus Christ, who was I that I could stand in God's way.' When they heard this, <u>they quieted down and glorified God</u> saying, 'Well then, God has granted to the Gentiles also the repentance that leads to life** (Acts 11:16-18).'" (Emphasis mine)

THE PRIMARY PURPOSE

There is that interesting and I believe significant statement found in verse 18 of Acts chapter 11, **"they quieted down ..."**

That seems to imply that the Jewish believers in Jerusalem, to whom Peter is reporting, are not at all happy about the possibility of Gentiles being welcomed into the Church of Christ. But that which made the difference was the report that the obvious and manifest gift of tongues had been observed, not only by Peter, but by the Jewish believers from Jerusalem who were there and saw it all. Note verse 45 of Acts chapter10, **"All the circumcised believers who came with Peter were amazed, because the gift of the Holy Spirit had been poured out on the Gentiles also."**

Now we note again what Peter said to them as found in verses 16-17 of Acts 11, **"And I remembered the word of the Lord, how He used to say, 'John baptized with water, but you will be baptized with the Holy Spirit.' Therefore, if God gave to them the same gift as *He gave* to us also after believing in the Lord Jesus Christ, who was I to stand in God's way?"** How do you convince the Jews of those days that Gentiles, who were inherently unclean in their minds, are to be included in the fellowship of Christ? It would have to be something very powerful and convincing. The dramatic gift of speaking in tongues was designed to be very convincing. That I believe was the primary purpose of the sign gift that we saw in Acts chapter 2 and then see in the house of Cornelius.

At the end of our consideration of the Ethiopian eunuch we read that he **"went on his way rejoicing (Acts 8:39)."** I would imagine that there was much rejoicing in the household of the Roman commander as well, after they had responded to the Gospel message and received the blessing of the Spirit of God. That kind of joy, I believe, is very often the case in the aftermath of God's special appointments.

CHAPTER THREE

THE WRONG HOTEL

MINSK, BELARUS-- ca. 2002 A.D.

She sat behind a desk, a few feet from the elevator doors on the 9th floor of the hotel. Unlike many who sat behind desks in this former Soviet republic, she seemed to be quite cheerful, friendly and helpful. The maids on that floor rotated in that position behind the desk, handing out large wooden key holders to the people who were returning to their rooms. As you left your room and went down the hall to the elevators, you would leave your key with the maid there. It was too large to carry with you anyway. One day when I was at the elevator doors, deciding which button to push, she came over with a big smile on her face as if to help me do the right thing. Let's assume her name is Tanya, a good Russian name.

However, I was in the wrong hotel, that is with respect to where I thought I would be on this, my seventh trip to teach at a Bible College in Minsk. I taught the same course each time. It was a doctrinal survey course covering the theological divisions: "Sin, Salvation, The Church and Last Things." It was a situation where you taught the same course all day long for two weeks. In all, as I stated on an earlier page, I spend about 50 hours with the students each time I went there. I believe I stayed in three different hotels during the course of those years. Usually though, we stayed in one particular hotel. This year, three other pastors and I had reservations at the hotel where we expected to be.

However, when we arrived, we found that things had changed. The president/dictator of that country decided that he needed those rooms for a government conference. The managers of the hotel had no choice. The Christian organization now called "Cru," at the last moment, made reservations for us at a hotel across the river (the Svislach) not too far away. It was a little disappointing at first. We knew our way around the hotel where we expected to be. We had become quite familiar with those surroundings. The Communist president who controlled that hotel had made his plans. But our wise God had made His own plans. I was to find out that He had set up an appointment for me to meet someone in another hotel, the one across the river.

As time went by that first week, my casual friendship with Tanya grew. One Sunday morning she was at the desk when I arrived at the elevators, dressed up in suit and tie, briefcase in hand, ready to speak in one of the Baptist churches in the city. She gave me a big smile and a thumbs up as I started for the open door of the elevator. I don't think she had any idea where

I was going or what I was doing in the city. I could not speak with her because I could not speak Russian well enough to have a meaningful conversation and she could not speak English.

Later as I was resting in my hotel room. I thought of the fact that I had brought with me from the U.S. a number of T-shirts. I always brought gifts from America for my students and this time, after giving them out, I had three T-shirts left.

I thought of Tanya. "I wonder if she has kids and I wonder if she would like to have them." I walked down the hallway and saw Tanya at the desk. (She wasn't always there. As I mentioned the maids of the floor rotated to that position.) By means of gestures I was able to communicate my question. "Do you have children"? She nodded yes. Then I held the shirts out to her as if you say, "Would you like to have these.? She nodded yes, with a big happy smile and then she came around the desk and kissed me on the cheek. I should mention that at the time I was about 67 years old. (Like a grand-pa)

I went back to my room and began to think of how I might speak to her about Jesus. But there was that language barrier. I then began to seriously pray for her. I felt burdened of the Spirit to do so. When I was back in seminary, I read a book by Lewis Sperry Chafer entitled "True Evangelism." The repeated message of that book is, "*We need to speak with God about people before we speak to people about God.*" At the time I wasn't remembering the message of that book, I just knew that I needed to pray for Tanya.

After a while, I believe, the Lord led me to think this way:

Next Sunday I will have an interpreter with me as I go to speak at another church. In the morning she will meet me in the hotel lobby and then take me by means of bus, trolly, whatever, to the church. Perhaps, we will go back for dinner at the pastor's house afterwards. Then Elena, (let's call her Elena) will bring me back to the hotel. I will ask her to wait in the lobby while I go up to the ninth floor. If Tanya is at the desk, I will come back down to the lobby and have Elena come back to my floor and together we will have a conversation with Tanya. It seemed like it might work. But what if Tanya is not at the desk that day?

Sunday came. I put on suit and tie and walked down the hall to the elevators. Much to my disappointment Tanya was not there. I turned in my key to the maid who was there and went downstairs to meet my interpreter, Elena. Later that day after church and after dinner at the pastor's house we returned to the hotel about mid-afternoon. I asked Elena to wait in the lobby while I went to see if Tanya was at the desk on the nineth floor. Wonderful! She was there on this Sunday afternoon. After I retrieved Elena from the lobby, we were able to speak with Tanya. She soon found out who I was and what I was doing in Minsk. She said, "Yes, I went to church one time. I think it was Baptist. I liked it." After a while she told us that she had a college-age daughter. Let's say her name was Yulia. Tanya said that Yulia was studying English and would like very much to go to America and study there. Tanya wanted to know if we could get together with Yulia. This was Sunday and I was due to fly home on Thursday. There was not much time, but we settled on Wednesday afternoon as a time to meet. Wednesday came and Tanya arrived with her daughter. I must confess that I had hoped Yulia would not come. I wanted to talk with Tanya about Christ. I didn't want to talk with a young person about going to America. I was soon to learn how wrong I was about that. The Lord knew best. We had intended to meet at a picnic table located near the hotel. However, it was extremely windy. Too windy to speak with each other over the pages of a Bible blowing in the wind. It seemed there was only one place to meet, in my room on the ninth floor. Tanya chose to go up a back way so that she would not be seen coming to my room. So, there we sat, the four of us, in my hotel room, Tanya, Yulia, Elena, and myself.

Right at the beginning Yulia began by telling me that a few years ago there was a man from Texas who came to speak somewhere in the city. She said that she had made some kind of a decision for God, but she wasn't sure just what it was about. So, the person I had hoped would not be there was the key to our meeting. It was Yulia who had been sending up the positive signals to God. So, my appointment, at the wrong hotel, was with two people, not just one.

I shared the gospel with these two women and said to Yulia, "Let's try and clarify what kind of a decision a person needs to make in order to become a true believer in Jesus Christ. Would you like to pray with me a prayer of faith, just to make sure about this?" She said, "yes." Then I turned to Tanya and asked, "Would you like to do this too?" She said, "yes." I said, "wonderful, let's pray together, please repeat after me."

So, I said "Lord Jesus, thank you for your love," And Elena repeated in Russian, "Lord Jesus, thank you for your love," And then the two women prayed in Russian, "Lord Jesus, thank you for your love." And so, it went: I said, "Thank you for dying on the cross for my sins," Elena, in Russian, "Thank you for dying for my sins." The two women, "Thank you for dying on the cross for my sins." And so, it went until their faith in Christ had been affirmed. "I believe in you, I want to receive you into my heart, …" How dramatic and wonderful that was for me in those moments. Here I was, in the wrong hotel, not being able to speak Russian, knowing that my Lord God had put all this together. No, actually, I was in the right hotel, at the right time, the right girl was there in spite of my thinking and the language barrier was no problem at all.

That evening I went to the circus. The staff at the school endeavored to provide entertainment for the pastors who were there by scheduling events for us to attend like concerts, ballet, opera, etc. It was not at all costly because of the value of the American dollar compared to that of Belarus. I enjoyed concerts by their symphony orchestra and Bolshoi Ballet presentations like "Swan Lake." But tonight, it was the circus. It was very good, well done, but I didn't enjoy it very much. The fun at watching the circus performers could not compare with the joy that I felt with respect to what had happened that afternoon. There was just no comparison. The circus for me that evening was dull and mundane.

At home, a few weeks later I wrote Tanya and Yulia a

letter. The next year they told me that they had received my letter but were afraid to write back. They were afraid of the communists in control, that they would react adversely to communications with Americans. That year I spent some time with them having, this time, a different interpreter. It went fairly well. I found out that Tanya had a son who was in prison. We prayed for him. It is my assurance that I will see them some day before the Throne of Grace. In the meantime, I rest assured that the Holy Spirit will look after them and provide for them the Christian fellowship that they need. If the Lord sent me to meet with them, then He can send others to help them along the way. Note: I did try to connect them to the Bible college where I was teaching, but as I recall, that did not work out.

MY BONNIE LIVES OVER THE OCEAN

(Dear reader, if you do not want to read more about myself at this point. I understand. You may of course jump ahead to the beginning of the next chapter. The following happened to me on the same day that I met with Tanya and Yulia at the hotel.)

When I began to embark on my seventh trip to Minsk, Belarus, I prayed like this: "Lord, how long should I continue to do this, traveling almost every year to teach at the Bible School in Minsk? When will it be enough? This will be trip number seven. I know that in the Bible seven is the number that indicates completion. The people at church have faithfully supported this missionary endeavor. Is this the final trip? Lord, could you please give me some indication as to when I should stop?"

I flew to Europe having these thoughts in mind. My class that year was small compared to some of the others I had had. During the session one day I thought I would have a little fun with them. I wrote on the white board the words to an old song: "My Bonnie Lies Over the Ocean." They learned the song very quickly, since they enjoyed any challenge to learn a little English. I had done this in the past at a men's retreat and I know others have done it to give people a little exercise. While I played a guitar and led the singing, they were to sing it a certain way: I said, "Every time we come to a word that begins with the letter B you must stand up. The next time we come to a word that begins with the letter B, sit down. Continue this until we get to the end of the song." Of course, since for the most part they were college age young people, standing up and sitting down repeatedly was no problem. I made the excuse that since I was playing the guitar, I could not stand and sit through the song. The song looks like this:

My Bonnie lies over the ocean, My Bonnie lies over the sea, My Bonnie lies over the ocean, oh Bring Back my Bonnie to me.

Bring Back, Bring Back, oh Bring Back my Bonnie to me to me, Bring Back, oh Bring Back, oh Bring Back my Bonnie to me.

If done correctly, everyone should be sitting when the song

is over. We did this little exercise several times. I think they enjoyed it.

After the two-week period of classes was over, the school scheduled a closing program after lunch on Wednesday. The final exams had taken place just before lunch. There were four pastors who had come to teach at the school for that session and each class said goodbye to their teachers with some kind of speech, song, or skit. When my class got up to present what they had prepared I thought they were going to sing the song I had taught them. But what they did was like cupid's arrow in my heart. They changed the words. The sang it like this:

My teacher lives over the ocean, my teacher lives over the sea, My teacher lives over the ocean, oh bring back my teacher to me. Bring back, bring back, oh bring back my teacher to me to me, bring back, oh bring back, oh bring back my teacher to me!

They prepared it in English and I doubt that they really understood what impact it had on me at that moment. I think the Lord was telling me, "Yes, you need to come back next year." After that, on that same afternoon, I went back to the hotel with Elena, my interpreter, to meet Tanya and Yulia and pray with them to trust in Christ. Those two events together said to me, "You should come back."

CHAPTER FOUR

DOWN BY THE RIVERSIDE

Part One

THE BUSINESS WOMAN

She came to a place beside a river and sat down with a group of women wanting, perhaps, to pray and worship God with them. Her name was Lydia. Unknown to her at the time was the fact that she was on God's Appointment Calendar. One of God's servants was on the way.

She would not be famous like Deborah the Judge, or Esther the Queen, or Ruth the Moabite, or Hannah, or Rahab, or the special follower of Jesus who was well known, Mary from Magdala. We could mention more. But she was to become highly regarded by the people of Philippi as well as by the apostle Paul. She was to have a very important role in the work of Paul on his second missionary journey. She is mentioned in only three verses in chapter 16 of the book of Acts:

"A woman named Lydia, from the city of Thyatira, a seller of purple fabrics, a worshipper of God, was listening; and the Lord opened her heart to respond to the things spoken by God. And when she and her household had been baptized, she urged us saying, 'If you have judged me to be faithful to the Lord, come into my house and stay.' And she prevailed upon us, …They went out of the prison and entered the house of Lydia, and when they saw the brethren, they encouraged them and departed (Acts 16:14,15, 40)."

The account is very brief. We read that she was from Thyatira, a city in Proconsular Asia that was known for the manufacture and sale of purple fabrics. Apparently, she was here on business. She was from Thyatira, but she occupied a house in Philippi large enough to extend hospitality to Paul, Timothy, Luke and possibly Silas, as well as care for her own family and probably servants. Several commentators which I have read indicate that her household, like that of Cornelius of which I wrote before, was large enough to include servants. That would seem to indicate that she was a rather successful business-woman. She was a woman of means. When Paul later wrote to them his letter we know as Philippians, he does not mention her. Perhaps she had returned to Thyatira, her business in Philippi concluded. Her house was to become important vantage ground, or base of operations, for Paul's work in Philippi.

The place where the women were gathered is called in verse 13 of Acts 16 "a place of prayer." G. Campbell Morgan states, "'The place of prayer' is a technical phrase. Jewish places of prayer were found throughout all these cities, where no synagogues were built" [G. Campbell Morgan, p. 380]. When the apostle Paul arrived in a new city, he usually went to a synagogue on the first sabbath after his arrival. Here we read, **"and on the Sabbath day we went outside the gate to a riverside, where we were supposing there would be a place of prayer... (Acts 16:13)."**

A number of commentators suggest that apparently there was no synagogue in the city. It seems that the existence of a synagogue required that there be at least ten Jewish men in the city.

F.F. Bruce in his commentary on Acts quotes Rabbi Halafta Ben Dosa, of the village of Hanayana who said, "When ten people sit together and occupy themselves with the Torah, the *Shekhinah* abides among them, as it is said, "God standeth in the synagogue of God"' [F.F. Bruce, p. 331].

The fact that we read of these women gathered in a place of prayer has great significance with respect to the opening verse of Psalm 137, '**By the rivers of Babylon, there we sat down, yea, we wept. (Psalm 137:1).'"** [G. Campbell Morgan, p. 381]

This says something also of Lydia. She sat down with these

Hebrew women and we read that she was "**a worshipper of God.**" Acts 16:14. That is to say she is moving toward the true God before God's servant arrives to explain the Gospel of Jesus to her. Furthermore, she has an affinity toward the Jewish people. She is worshipping the one true God of Israel with these Hebrew women. We saw in our consideration of the Ethiopian Eunuch that he had been to Jerusalem and had obtained a copy of the book of Isaiah. This was also true of the Roman centurion, Cornelius, who gave alms to the Jewish people. Again, we are reminded of Genesis 12:3, where God promised the father of the Jewish people, "**And I will bless those who bless you …**".

Let us now leave Lydia waiting by the river-side and consider the second missionary journey of the apostle Paul, who through some difficulty is on the way to Philippi.

THE MACEDONIAN VISION

Paul has begun his second missionary journey which would take him to a number of new cities, cities that he had not served in before, which were: Philippi, Thessalonica, Berea, Athens, and Corinth. But first he would revisit some of the places where he had been on his first missionary journey. He was to pick up Timothy in Lystra and later on he would meet and enlist Luke in Troas. By the time they would arrive in Philippi there would be Silas, Timothy, and Luke traveling with him.

But things were not going smoothly. Right at the beginning,

as they were making plans for the journey, there was a major disagreement with Barnabas. That is recorded in Acts 15:36-40. We read in verse 39 and 40 of Acts chapter 15, **"And there occurred such a sharp disagreement that they separated from one another, and Barnabas took Mark with him and sailed away to Cyprus, but Paul chose Silas and left, being committed by the brethren to the grace of the Lord."**

That would not seem to be a good beginning. Many commentators have taken sides on this contention between the two. Some say Barnabas was right. Others insist that Paul was right in not wanting to take along John Mark who had failed them before. Nevertheless, that major incident must have burdened the mind and heart of Paul as he took Silas with him to begin the long journey.

His second major disagreement was with the Lord. Paul wanted to revisit the places where he had been before and thus, strengthen the saints for their further ministry. Then he would go to some new places in that area known to us now as Asia Minor. As far as we know he had no intention at all of going to Europe, but that's where the Lord would eventually take him.

We read in chapter 16 of the difficulties that Paul had with the Lord: **"So the churches were being strengthened in the faith, and were increasing in number daily. They passed through the Phrygian and Galatian region, <u>having been forbidden</u> by the Holy Spirit to speak the word in Asia,** (*Emphasis mine*) **and as they came to Mysia, they were trying**

to go into Bithynia, and the <u>Spirit of Jesus did not permit</u> them (Acts 16:5-9)." (Emphasis mine).

Generally speaking, Paul kept trying to go north and east, while the Lord wants them to go west. Finally, in verses 9-10 of Acts chapter 16 we learn of the Macedonian vision: **"A vision appeared to Paul in the night: a man of Macedonia was standing and appealing to him, and saying, 'Come over to Macedonia and help us.' When he had seen the vision, immediately we sought to go into Macedonia, concluding that God has called us to preach the gospel to them (Acts 16:9-10)."** Many have speculated as to the identity of the man in the vision.

I lean to the view that it was an angel that Paul saw. Back in Acts chapter 8 we read that an angel of the Lord instructed Philip to go south to the Gaza strip area. A few verses later we read that the Spirit told him to "Go and join this chariot" (Acts 8:29). Likewise, in chapter 10 of Acts verse 3 we read of Cornelius **"About the ninth hour of the day he clearly saw in a vision an angel of God who had just come in ..."** Later in the chapter Peter hears the voice of the Lord and has a vision of a great sheet coming down from Heaven. (Acts 10:11) But then in verse 19 of Acts chapter 10 we read, **"While Peter was reflecting on the vision, the Spirit said to him, 'Behold three men are looking for you."** So, in the two passages that I have mentioned, there is both a reference to an angel and also a reference to the Spirit. I think we probably have the same here. There is a reference to the Spirit in verses 6 and 7 of Acts

16. Therefore, it's perhaps an angel that speaks to him in the Macedonian vision.

But now the question is, how is Paul guided in these circumstances?

PAUL AND THE HOLY SPIRIT

Let us now focus on verses 6 and 7 of Acts chapter 16 where we read of Paul struggling to know and follow God's plans for his missionary journey. It seems that it wasn't easy. In verse 6 of Acts chapter 16 the language sounds harsh, he was **"forbidden by the Holy Spirit to speak the word in Asia."** When we look into the matter, we find that the situation was harsher than we might have thought. We read that after the Holy Spirit so dealt with them, they **"passed through the Phrygian and Galatian region (Acts 16:6)."**

Paul's letter to the church in Galatia brings light to the situation. We have the following verses taken from chapter four of that book: **"...You have done me no wrong; but you know that it was because of a bodily illness that I preached the gospel to you the first time; and that which was a trial to you in my bodily condition you did not despise or loathe, but you received me as an angel of God, as Christ Himself** (Galatians 4:12-14)."

This is a remarkable revelation. The reason why Paul did not take his group into Asia, as he intended to do, was because he became very ill. We cannot imagine what the problem was.

Was it his "thorn in the flesh," that we read of in II Cor. 12:7, that he is referring to, or something else? Whatever it was, it was quite serious. Notice again what Paul says in Gal 4:14, **"that which was a trial to you in my bodily condition you did not <u>despise or loath</u>, ..."** (Emphasis mine) The "trial" that he speaks of is not his trial, although it was one for him. Rather, Paul's horrible condition was a trial that they had to endure. It sounds like it was something quite repulsive. Was he hard to look at in his condition, or hard to listen to? We can only imagine. Thankfully, the Galatians passed the test. In spite of his condition, they received him as **"an angel of God... (Gal. 4:14)."**

Our point here is this: God used severe illness to steer His apostle in the right direction. Concerning his "thorn in the flesh" that we mentioned above, Paul in that verse (II Cor. 12:7), says that it was **"a messenger of Satan to torment me."** Just as is taught in the book of Job, sometimes our God allows Satan to inflict us, for His sovereign purpose.

Back in Acts 16:6 we just read that they were **"forbidden by the Holy Spirit to speak the word in Asia."** We don't know the details as to how the Spirit of God directed him to go in one direction and not another. We do not have to imagine that the Spirit spoke to him verbally. In fact, I cannot think of any place in Scripture where the Spirit so speaks. There are dreams and visions or an appearance of an angel of the Lord. In the Christmas story it is always an angel sent by God to communicate a message. Rather, the Holy Spirit speaks to us on a spiritual level. And we can realize that today. As I said, it is difficult to know just how the Holy Spirit made known to Paul God's will, as Paul is struggling with this illness. Was it mainly circumstantial? In the case just discussed, apparently it was impossible for Paul to travel into Proconsul Asia with the afflictions and illness that he was enduring. He would have to turn aside for rest and quietness. A while later he went to the region of Galatia.

THE SPIRIT OF JESUS

Nowhere else in the Bible do we have this phrase. Paul does speak of the "Spirit of Christ in Romans chapter 8, verse 9: **"However, you are not in the flesh but in the Spirit, if indeed the Spirit of God dwells within you. But if anyone does not have the Spirit of Christ, he does not belong to Him."** Reading this verse, it is easy to conclude that the Spirit of God and Spirit of Christ are one and the same. It is also easy to conclude that the term "Spirit of Jesus" is one with the Spirit of God. Throughout the book of Acts Luke has been speaking of the Holy Spirit as active and guiding the lives of the disciples of Christ. Why then does he speak of the "Spirit of Jesus"? It seems to me that there is a deliberate contrast made between the terms used in verse 6 of Acts chapter16 and verse 7. In the one there is harshness. In the other there is the tender touch of the love of Jesus. In II Corinthians 5:14, **"For the love of Christ controls us, having concluded this, that one died for**

all, therefore all died." The man who walked on this earth and taught us about the love of God and then hung on a cross for our sins, His name is Jesus. I suggest therefore, that the Holy Spirit is presenting to Paul a picture of Jesus and His love in this situation. We just don't know what exactly is happening as Paul is under the influence of the Holy Spirit. We just read, **"...they were trying to go into Bithynia, and the Spirit of Jesus did not permit them (Acts 16:7)."** Somehow, they are influenced by the love of Jesus in the Spirit.

(Note: Please see Appendix for an essay on decision making and will of God for our day.)

SMOOTH SAILING

They went down to Troas, where they picked up Luke, and then, at that point, there is the vision of the man of Macedonia who is calling them to the West and Europe. And after that, the will of God now having become clear, it was smooth sailing.

"So, putting out to sea from Troas, we ran a straight course to Samothrace, and on the day following to Neapolis" **(Acts 16:11).** Neapolis was the seaport for Philippi, which was just a few miles away. Running a "straight course" is a way of saying they had the wind behind them. Sailors today speak of having a "following sea." The wind was behind them. They sailed to Neapolis in just two days. Later, in Acts, we read that on another occasion the same trip took five days.

PAUL IN PHILIPPI

"And on the Sabbath day we went outside the gate to a riverside, where we were supposing that there would be a place of prayer, and we sat down and began speaking to the women who had assembled (Acts 16:13)." We notice the occurrence of the word "we". It is found three times in this verse. Luke is the human author of the book of Acts, and since he joined Paul and the others in Troas, he includes himself in the narrative. He says, "We."

G. Campbell Morgan makes this observation at this point, "Paul was a Pharisee, who through the long years of his early life had repeated such words as these, 'O God, I thank Thee that I am neither Gentile nor slave, nor woman.' The man who presently wrote, 'in Christ there is neither Jew nor Gentile, bond, nor free, male nor female,' thus contradicted the false view of the thanksgiving that had passed his lips for years. He now abandoned the Pharisaic contempt for a woman. The apostle of Jesus Christ found no man in the place of prayer, but the old contempt was gone, and to the women assembled, he spoke. He dared to do so because the Gospel had changed his intellectual conception, and entirely transformed him" [Morgan p. 381 and 382)] We might add that Paul usually stood while teaching, but now he sits with these women. He might even have thought of the time when Jesus sat by a well in Samaria and had that wonderful conversation with a Samaritan woman. He is doing now what Christ would do.

"A woman named Lydia, from the city of Thyatira, a seller of purple fabrics, a worshipper of God, was listening; and the Lord opened her heart to respond to the things spoken by Paul (Acts 16:14)." We now notice two or three matters found in this verse to be considered: First, we read that she was a "**worshipper of God (Acts 16:14**." We believe that this means she was moving toward God in her own response to the light she had at the time. She was sending up the positive signals that we spoke about. In a pagan world where people were worshiping many gods, she worshipped the one true God, the God of Israel. In a former chapter we mentioned two possibilities in this regard. She could have been a proselyte to Judaism or she might have been what the Jews referred to as a "God fearer." If she was a proselyte, she would have been endeavoring to keep all of the laws and precepts of the Torah. In my view of her, I lean to the latter. She was listening, learning and praying to the one whom she believed to be the one true God. Importantly, she is responding in a positive way to the light that she had. In verse 14 of Acts chapter 16 it says, **"she was listening… to the things spoken by Paul**."

The second thing we see in verse 14 of Acts 16 is that "**the Lord opened her heart.**" That is to say, the Holy Spirit was at that point acting upon her heart. Here again we have that tension between the two realities mentioned before. On the one hand we have the words of John 7:17, **"If anyone is willing to do His will, he will know of the teaching, whether it is of God or *whether* I speak from Myself.**" On the other hand, we have the words of Christ in John 6:44, "**No one can come to Me unless the Father who sent Me, draws him; ...**" She was listening, but God opened her heart.

(Dear reader, please refer to an appendix at the end of this writing for a brief discussion of election and free will.)

In verse 15 of Acts chapter 16 we also have two notable things. The next thing for Lydia and her household was Baptism. We observe that with regard to all of the persons we have considered; the Ethiopian, Cornelius and now Lydia, first there is faith and then there is Baptism. Furthermore, Lydia seems to have been somewhat like Cornelius. She has had a godly influence upon all those living in her house. All her household, family and servants were ready to go through the waters of Baptism. We don't have to assume that there were very small children involved. It would seem that she was a "woman of means" as is implied in the passage. Which probably means she is not 18 or 20 years of age or an older young adult. She is more likely to have been "middle-aged." Of course, we don't know. Furthermore, many commentators believe she was a widow.

We also notice in Acts 16:15. She says, "**...If you have judged me to be faithful to the Lord, come into my house and stay. She prevailed upon us.**" Her manner of speech here would seem to indicate humility. "If I seem to be worthy of it, would you consider coming to stay in my house?" We notice also that there is implied a passage of time. Apparently, she and her household were not baptized immediately, as was the case with the Ethiopian eunuch. **"If you have judged me to be faithful..."** (Acts 16:15) Paul would need some time to do that, more than a few minutes.

We can imagine that this special woman, after listening to Paul and coming to saving faith, went home and began to evangelize, not only her family, but her servants and whatever assistants were involved in her business. Apparently, she was very successful in sharing her faith, because her entire household was baptized with her. Perhaps that event took place on the following Sabbath. Was Paul involved in this during that interval? Did he come to her house and speak to the members of her household? Perhaps. We don't know.

SHE CONSTRAINED US

Those are the words of the King Version of the Bible. The New American Standard reads, **"She prevailed upon us (Acts 16:15)."** The Greek word used here is rare in Scripture. It occurs twice, both times penned by Luke. In the Gospel of Luke, we have the account of the post-resurrection appearance of Jesus when He walked with two disciples on the way to Emmaus. We read in Luke 24:28-29, **"And they approached the village where they were going, and He acted as though He were going farther. But they urged Him, [constrained in the KJV] saying, stay with us, for it is getting toward evening, and the day is nearly over. So, He went in to stay with them."** The occurrence of the same word is found here in Acts 16:15.

According to Carter and Earle in their commentary on Acts, [page 235], the literal force of the word "parabiazamai," is "to force against nature or law." In the classics it meant "to compel by force." Not so strong in the Greek of the New Testament, it reads "to constrain by entreaty." Carter and Earle take it as meaning a "vehement urgency of the feeling of gratitude." Therefore, I am happy with the rendering of the New American Standard version, "she prevailed upon us." In her gratitude she was very insistent that Paul and his companions stay in her house. It was a gracious, but compelling invitation. I referenced the Greek connotation of the word to show something of the strength that the word denotes. She constrained us, or "**prevailed upon us (Acts 16:15).**" It was a strong, but good invitation to stay in her house.

VANTAGE GROUND

G. Campbell Morgan emphasizes in his work on the book of Acts that this house in Philippi was very important concerning the cause of the Gospel in Philippi. G. Campbell Morgan writes the following, "So, a house was opened to Jesus in Philippi. Christ needs vantage ground in Philippi, on which He can stand, and proclaim His evangel, from which He can send His messengers forth to capture the city, and all the region beyond, for Himself. He finds a woman's heart and a woman's house" [Morgan, page 382]. He then refers us to Philippians 1:3-5, **"I thank my God in all my remembrance of you,** always offering prayer with joy in my every prayer for you all, in view of your participation in the gospel from the first day until now." Morgan then asks "What was that "first day"? The day when Lydia's heart was opened" [Morgan, page 383]

Morgan then quotes Philippians 4:15-16, **"You yourselves also know, Philippians, that at the first preaching of the gospel, after I left Macedonia, no church shared with me in the matter of giving and receiving but you alone, for even in Thessalonica you sent a *gift* more than once for my needs."**

Morgan says, "There was gathered in Philippi a fellowship of souls, that Paul always seems to have looked upon as the chief joy and crown of his ministry…The church in Philippi was evidently most dear to him. Thus, in Philippi there was a growing fellowship of faithful souls, a base of operation widening and broadening, ever helping this man with his work. This began when Lydia's heart was opened, she opened her home for Jesus Christ" [Morgan, page 38].

We want to emphasize that this story begins before the arrival of Paul in this important city; it began when she began to seek God with all her heart. The Holy Spirit was at work in her heart as well in that of the apostle Paul. Lydia is one of the notable women of the Bible.

CHAPTER FIVE

DOWN BY THE RIVERSIDE

Part Two

MINSK, BELARUS – 1995 A.D.

She sat near the bank of the Svislach, the beautiful river that runs from north-west to southeast right through the city of Minsk. It was a very warm day, above average for the month of May in Belarus. People were everywhere, walking by the river, swimming in the river, sitting or lying on the grass so as to catch the rays of the warm sun on this Saturday afternoon. She was perhaps ten years old, enjoying the day as she sat on a blanket with her father and mother. She thinks she sees an American tourist. He is standing nearby in the shade of a small tree and holding a camera. "He looks like an American," she thinks, "with that camera and baseball cap."

She looks at him so as to catch his eye and when she does, she lifts her voice and says slowly and deliberately "HELLO! HOW ARE YOU?" The man smiles and says back to her, "I

AM FINE, HOW ARE YOU?" The young girl, let's assume her name is Elena, wants to try out the little bit of English she has learned. And thus, began a meaningful friendship that was to last for some time.

BACK TO THE BEGINNING

It was my first short-term missionary trip to the city of Minsk. This capital city of Belarus, located in the center of that former Soviet country, consists of almost two million people. They have their own language, which is similar to Russian, but while under Soviet control everyone was influenced to learn Russian. It was taught in the schools during the Soviet era and so in reality many people there speak Russian as well as Belarussian. It was not difficult for me to adapt to teaching with the aid of an interpreter. During that first year of teaching theology in the Evangelical Bible College there, as it was called, my interpreter was a young man who, I think, wanted to show off his interpreting skill. He spoke Russian simultaneously with me to the students as I was speaking to them in English. That is to say, we were both speaking always at the same time. Indeed, that was for me somewhat distracting. Happily, in the years that followed, I had interpreters who followed a much simpler method. I would say a sentence or two in English and then the interpreter conveyed to the students in Russian what I had said. Sometimes I had a class of students where one or two would know English. That made for an interesting event. If I told a joke, the few students who knew English would laugh and that was before the interpreter delivered the punch line in Russian so that the rest of the class could laugh. However, I should say that my time with these wonderful college age young people was very enjoyable. They were hungry to learn spiritual truth. I found that being already involved in church life there, they knew the history, the story and the details of the books of the Bible. But what they needed was to be versed in sound theology. How does it all fit together theologically? They were anxious to learn. That made for me a very enjoyable teaching experience.

THE INVITATION

On a certain day I was presenting the doctrines of the two ordinances of church life, Communion and Baptism. After my lecture on the practice of Baptism, some students came up to me and said, "Our church is having a baptismal service down at the river this coming Saturday afternoon. Would you like to come see it?"

I told them that I would very much like to come and be with them, however, I said to them, "Another pastor and myself have been invited to go out to visit with some people at their dacha (like a summer cottage) out in the country this Saturday. Therefore, I doubt that I can make it to your service of baptism., But if we get back in time I would like to come."

So, these students happily wrote out directions on how to get there by means of bus, metro (subway) and bus again.

CHANGE OF PLANS

My pastor-friend and I waited for the car to come which would take us to the dacha in the country as planned. We were looking forward to that occasion. But nine o'clock came, then ten o'clock, eleven o'clock, still no one came to pick us up. Finally, around noon we decided that we might as well go to the river location and observe the baptismal service. We later learned that the people who were supposed to pick us up had a last-minute problem with their vehicle and thus could not come. We had the directions. So, we took a bus, then the metro (subway) and then another bus and finally arrived at the destination. But no one from the school was there.

We decided to walk along the river and watch for any signs of Christians getting ready to enjoy the planned event. We walked and then walked some more. We found no one and could not speak with any one because we did not have an interpreter with us. We turned around and walked back along the river. Almost giving up hope we saw a group of people walking across the field from the bus stop. They were in street clothes. "Yes," we surmised. This must be the church group.

We waited and watched as they proceeded to set up a tent. The candidates for the event would change clothes there in preparation for experiencing the waters of Baptism. That is when the young girl, wanting to try out her English, caught my eye and said, "HOW ARE YOU?"

She and her family warmly waved me over to where they were and insisted that I join them on the small blanket upon which they were sitting. I tried to resist--it was a very small blanket, but they insisted. They seemed to be very friendly, but of course we could not talk because of the language barrier. But the little girl tried. She said, slowly and deliberately, "We live in America." I said, "Oh, you went to America?" But she was confusing her pronouns. She meant to say, "You live in America?" And so, it went. We could do not much more than smile at each other. I called my pastor-friend over, but things did not change. Through all of this I was wishing that I could tell this little girl about Jesus and His love. But I could not.

Eventually, Sergei, the father (Let's assume that their names were Sergei, Tamara and Elena- also very common Russian names), gave me a business card. Later we learned that it indicated that he was the director of an electronics firm in Minsk. On the back of the card, he wrote their home address and phone number and somehow expressed to me that I should come and visit them sometime. Very soon after that they got up and left. I was very disappointed to see them go. I was enjoying their company. They didn't stay to watch the baptism. I don't imagine that they knew what it was all about anyway.

The next day, Sunday, I spoke in two churches. Throughout the day I thought a great deal about this family that I had met down by the riverside. Back at the school on Monday I spoke to one of the interpreters there, who throughout the day worked with the pastor-teachers, and asked her if she was free that evening. Let's say her name is Anya. She said yes. I asked her if she would come to the apartment where I lived and telephone a family that I had met on Saturday. She said that she would.

THE CALL

It took a little while for us to find a public phone that worked. At this point in time, right after the Iron Curtain came down, a lot of things in this former Soviet Republic did not work, and of course this was before the prevalence of cell phones. Anya called the number and said to Tamara who answered, "Do you remember the American that you met on Saturday?" She paused and then said "yes." Anya said, and I did not instruct her to say this, "He would like to know if he could come and see you this evening." There was then a long pause on the line and finally Tamara said, "Yes, it is sudden, but tell him to come. We will be waiting."

We gave the address to a Taxi driver and of course he knew exactly where to go. He drove us into the parking lot of what was a typical Soviet style apartment complex, tall buildings surrounding a central common grassy area used for recreational activity. Before our vehicle had come to a full stop someone was knocking on a side window. It was Elena, giving us a welcome. She had with her a little blond girl, a little shorter than Elena. I said to her "Kak vos zer voot?" (I knew a tiny bit of Russian)

That is to say, "What is your name?" She looked me in the eye and deliberately said, "MY NAME IS ELENA." So now I had two Elenas, two little girls who needed to know about Jesus.

IN THE APARTMENT

It was a very small apartment on the seventh floor of their building. There was a living room, a very small kitchen and the bedroom where Elena slept. Sergei and Tamara slept on a sofa bed in the living room. When we arrived, Sergei was not home. Tamara and Elena were very gracious. Elena went into her bedroom and brought out a number of paintings that she had created. She offered me one of my choosing as a gift to take back to America. It was wonderful that we could now speak with one another as I now had an interpreter. After a while Sergei came home and shortly after that there was a knock on the door. It was Tamara's father. I thought, "I don't want to talk to grandfather right now. I want to talk with these young people about Jesus." But he proved to be very nice. I had brought with me a pictorial church directory of my church in Massachusetts. Now they knew from that booklet who I was and what I did. They found it to be very interesting as they looked through the pages. I pointed out to them a picture of my daughter, her husband and my grand-children who attended the church.

THE BIBLE

After a while we were invited to go into the small kitchen for evening refreshments. When I thought it prudent to do so, I asked them about their church background. "Are you Greek Orthodox?" I forget exactly how I posed that question but Tamara said, "Yes." This then was the crucial moment. Tamara went somewhere and came back with a large Bible. She said that someone had given it to her in a park. She then told me that about a year previous she had had a serious problem with her heart. She said at that point, "<u>We began to seek God</u>." She went on to say that she and Sergei went to be married in a church. Apparently, they had been married under the Soviet seal. Now they wanted to bring God into their marriage.

DECISIONS

Anya, my interpreter, and I were in that home close to three hours. At the end of that time Tamara and Elena had made the decision to accept Christ as their Savior. Sergei, for himself and on behalf of Tamara's father said, "For men who have grown up in a Communist country, it is not easy to make such a decision." I urged them to continue to consider the matter, and let someone know when they had made a decision. As we prepared to leave the grandfather said, "Now, tomorrow night you must come to my house." So, the next night we went to visit Tamara's father and mother. We spent a good deal of time going through the Gospel of John with them. I left with them a Russian copy of a book written by Josh McDowel entitled, "More Than a Carpenter."

SERGEI

It took five years for Sergei to come to the place where he was ready to make a decision for Christ. My relationship with these people had developed to the place where they were pleased to have me stay with them while in Minsk, rather than in a hotel. As mentioned before, the staff at the school where I taught endeavored to provide entertainment for the American Pastors who were there. On this day they had given us tickets to a concert for that evening. That morning as I was riding in a taxi on the way to school, I said to myself, "No, I don't think I will go to the concert this evening. I believe I am supposed to stay in the apartment and talk to Sergei." I will not go into all the details as to what was happening in his life, but that evening Sergei did make a decision for Christ.

Now, I can tell you years later. Sergei became ill with Pancreatic Cancer. He is with the Lord.

LOOKING BACK

I remember well that night after that first evening with these people. Back at the dorm where I was staying at the time, I could not sleep. I was so filled with joy and wonderment concerning the whole matter. Here I was more than 3000 miles from home, again, at the wrong location, speaking the wrong language. I was supposed to be out in the country at someone's dacha. Rather I was down by the river where I could not speak with anyone because of the language barrier. Nevertheless, according to God's appointment calendar I was meant to be down by the riverside on that day.

In accordance with the theme of this writing I refer to the fact that Tamara came right out and said it that night in her kitchen. **"We began to seek God."**

CHAPTER SIX

BY WAY OF CONTRAST--
ROMANS ONE

We have been considering people, some from the book of Acts and some from my own experience, who chose to respond to the light that they had and began to seek more truth about the Creator. By way of contrast, we take note of what Paul says in Romans chapter one about men and women who have turned away from the light that they had. Paul says in Romans 1:18-25:

> **"For the wrath of God is revealed from heaven against all ungodliness and unrighteousness of men who suppress the truth in unrighteousness, because that which is known about God is evident within them; for God made it evident to them (Romans 1:18-19)."**

"For since the creation of the world His invisible attributes, His eternal power and divine nature have been clearly seen, being understood through what has been made, so that they are without excuse (Romans 1:20)."

"For even though they knew God, they did not honor Him as God or give thanks, but they became futile in their speculations, and their foolish heart was darkened. Professing to be wise, they became fools, and exchanged the glory of the incorruptible God for an image in the form of corruptible man and of birds and four-footed animals and crawling creatures (Romans 1:21-23)."

"Therefore, God gave them over in the lusts of their hearts to impurity, so that their bodies would be dishonored among them. For they exchanged the truth of God for a lie, and worshipped and served the creature rather than the Creator, who is blessed forever. Amen (Romans 1:24-25)." Below: please observe a diagram that depicts people responding to their creator in either- of two ways.

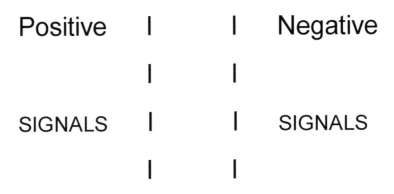

[The diagram above is from a lecture presented by Pastor Robert Thieme at Dallas Theological Seminary ca. 1960.]

On the above diagram the large V stands for "volition" or choice. Volition has a positive pole and a negative pole. Some people send up positive signals to God. They want more of God, more of His light. While others send up negative signals. "God, I don't want you in my life. I don't want more light. Just let me go my own way." We have been considering people who were sending up positive signals. In Romans chapter one Paul speaks about the people on this earth who have been and are now sending up negative signals. The diagram depicts signals going up to God, either from the negative pole or from the positive pole.

Paul's language in verses 18-24 of Romans one is very severe. **"For even though they knew God, they did not honor Him as God or give thanks, but they became futile in their speculations and their foolish heart was darkened."** He goes on to state the negative results of their negative signals. He speaks of the fact that they became futile or as the Greek can say, "empty" in their speculations. **"Their foolish heart was darkened (Rom. 1:21)."** That is to say, having turned away from the light, the darkness deepens.

Now we take note of the dire results of their choices. **"For this reason, God gave them over to degrading passions..."** (Rom. 1:26). Notice also verse 28 of Romans 1, **"And just as they did not see fit to acknowledge God any longer, God gave them over to a depraved mind, to do those things which are not proper."** After those words Paul goes into a long list (in verses 28-32 of Romans 1) of the many evils that have resulted from their choices.

Coming back to verse 18 of Romans one we read, **"For the wrath of God is revealed from heaven against all ungodliness and unrighteousness of men who <u>suppress the truth</u> in unrighteousness."** [Emphasis mine] Paul seems to be saying that God's wrath is revealed against them because they have made a choice to turn away from him. Did they then have free will to do so? God's wrath is against them because having the free will to do so, they suppressed the truth.

They turned away from the light that God had given them. Consequently, they descended into a deepening darkness to commit enumerable acts of ungodliness. (Which are listed in Rom.1:29-32)

What a contrast this is to the people we read of in the book of Acts who turned to the light that they were given.

By way of review, we considered the Ethiopian official who went to great lengths to travel many miles to worship in Jerusalem and obtain a copy of the Isaiah scroll. We then considered the Roman commander who was apparently a "God Fearer" who also gave alms to the Jewish people. After that we took note of the first convert in Europe, a business woman named Lydia who also worshipped God, met for prayer with a gathering of Jewish women down by the river in Philippi.

WHAT A CONTRAST!

Compare what we have studied about these people in the book of Acts to what God says about those who suppress the truth as stated in Romans chapter one. What a contrast!

As noted before the people we read of in Acts chapters 8, 9 and 16, have at least three things in common: Yes, they were all Gentiles. Secondly, concerning each of them there was an affinity for the chosen people, the Jews. And thirdly, more to the point of this writing, they are seeking to know more fully the one true God; and they do so before God's servants arrive on the scene. They had been placed on God's appointment calendar.

As we have been considering the several stories cited above, we bear in mind that sometimes that might not seem to be the case. I have in mind the conversion of the apostle Paul.

> **"Now Saul, still breathing threats and murder against the disciples of the Lord, went to the high priest, and asked for letters from him to the synagogues at Damascus, so that if he found any belonging to the Way, both men and women, he might bring them bound to Jerusalem. As he was traveling, it happened that he was approaching Damascus, and suddenly a light from heaven flashed around him; and he fell to the ground and heard a voice saying to him, 'Saul, Saul, why are you persecuting Me?' And he said, 'Who are You, Lord?' And He said, 'I am Jesus whom you are persecuting,' … (Acts 9:1-6)."**

The importance of Paul's experience is seen in the fact that it is recorded three times in the book of Acts, chapters 9, 22 and 26. The words of Paul in I Timothy 1:13 are interesting, **"even though I was formerly a blasphemer and a persecutor and a violent aggressor, yet I was shown mercy because I acted ignorantly in unbelief; and the grace of our Lord was more abundant, with the faith and love which was** *found* in Christ Jesus. It is a trustworthy statement, deserving full acceptance, that Christ Jesus came into the world to save sinners, among whom I am foremost. Yet for this reason I found mercy, so that in me as the foremost, Jesus Christ might demonstrate His perfect patience as an example for those who would believe in Him for eternal life (I Timothy 1:13-16)."

It seems therefore, that God in his grace and mercy must deal harshly with some so as to get them turned around. However, it is hard to say what was in Paul's mind leading up to that event on the road to Damascus. He says, that he found mercy with respect to what he had been doing and refers to himself as "**the foremost of sinners** (I Tim. 1:16)." But we have been considering people like the Ethiopian, Cornelius, Lydia and some of the people that I met in Minsk, Belarus. What I have been suggesting in this writing is that God could lead you to someone and use you to introduce a seeking person to Christ.

CHAPTER SEVEN

THE MEETING AT JACOB'S WELL

JOHN CHAPTER FOUR

She came alone, in the heat of the day. We read that it was the sixth hour, which was noon time according to Jewish timekeeping. She came alone, carrying a jug for water. He was alone sitting at the well, weary from His long walk from Judea. Apparently, He had insisted that his twelve friends all leave to go into town to buy food, otherwise, why would they all leave Him there alone in that hostile territory? On the other hand, if the woman saw from a distance thirteen men standing and sitting around the well, she might not have come to join such a group.

Let me say at the beginning of our consideration, I like this woman. This may come as a surprise to many because most of the commentators that I have read, suggest that she is an adulterous and promiscuous shameful woman. There are many negative descriptions of her to be found in the writings of Bible commentators. Apparently, these comments about her are made because we read that she has been married five times and is now living with a man who was not her husband. Rather, I believe she is a victim of the culture of the day and a victim of men in particular. Her's is a sad story, indeed. This was a day, when according to at least one Rabbinical school of thought (Hillel), a woman could be divorced for almost any reason at all. We have this referenced in Matthew 19:3, **"Some Pharisees came to Jesus, testing Him and asking 'Is it lawful for a man to divorce his wife for any reason at all?'"** Women were sometimes discarded for the slightest provocation. Perhaps, at first, she might go home to her parents. But after the second or third time, she is considered by many to be an immoral woman.

Nevertheless, this Samaritan woman was on God's appointment calendar. We read in the text that Jesus "**had to pass through Samaria** (John 4:4)." God the Father, was sending His Son to keep an appointment to meet with a Samaritan woman at Jacob's well near Sychar.

Scholars tell us that the feeling of hostility between the Jews and the people of Samaria was such that Jews would very often travel east, cross over the Jordan River, then head north where they could then head back west into Galilee. This might have been the case when Joseph and Mary traveled to Bethlehem. They perhaps went east, over the Jordan, so as to travel on the east side of the river, then travel south down to the point where they could head back over the river and west into Judea.

It was a much longer journey to go around that way because, as you might notice on a map of the area in New Testament times, Samaria was a fairly large province by comparison, much larger in area than Galilee. But Jesus was not going around, but going through that unfriendly territory because He had an appointment with a certain Samaritan woman, who I believe, was sending up some positive signals to God (Note the thoughts on that subject as found in the previous chapter).

A KEY VERSE

There are four words that are found in the New American Standard Version's translation of John 4:37 that cast significant light on this story. The verse reads, **"For in this case, the saying is true, 'One sows and another reaps (John 4:37).'"** {Emphasis mine] The English Standard Version has a similar rendering of the first part of John 4:37. This suggests to me, concerning this woman, that someone has shared the good news with her about Christ previous to her meeting with Jesus on this day. The seed had been sown and now Jesus is the One who with joy is reaping a soul for the Kingdom. How did that take place? Had she heard the preaching of John the Baptist, or heard the Good News from someone who had been a witness to his preaching? We read in John 3:23, **"John also was baptizing in Aenon near Salim, because there was much water there; and people were coming and were being baptized—for John had not yet been thrown into prison**

(John 3:23-24)." One can see on a map of the area that Aenon was not very far away from Sychar. It was on the west side of the Jordan, just within Samaritan territory. We don't know how or when, but the text seems to suggest that this woman had been exposed to the Good News of the Kingdom at some point prior to this meeting with Jesus at the well of Jacob.

NO EVIDENT NEGATIVE SIGNALS

She is asking questions, trying to understand what this stranger is all about. But I don't see negative signals in evidence. As the conversation between them proceeds she is not really resisting the hand of God reaching out to her.

> **"Jesus said to her, 'Give me a drink.' …Therefore, the Samaritan woman said to Him, 'How is it that You being a Jew, ask me for a drink since I am a Samaritan woman?' (For Jews have no dealing with Samarians.) Jesus answered and said to her, 'If you knew the gift of God, and who it is who says to you, "Give Me a drink," you would have asked Him, and He would have given you living water (John 4:9-10).'"**

She is surprised that He would speak with her, a Samaritan woman. It was unusual for a Jewish man to converse in this way with a woman and moreover, with a Samaritan woman. The Jews considered the Samaritans to be unclean and if a Jew drank or ate from a dish or vessel that a Samaritan had used, they too would become unclean. In II Kings chapter 17, verses 22-24 we read concerning the people who were living in that area: **"The sons of Israel walked in all the sins of Jeroboam which he did; they did not depart from them until the Lord removed Israel** (the ten northern tribes) **from His sight, as He spoke through all His servants the prophets. So, Israel was carried away from their own land to Assyria until this day. The king of Assyria brought** *men* **from Babylon and from Cuthah and from Avva and from Hamath and Sepharvaim, and settled** *them* **in the cities of Samaria in place of the sons of Israel. So, they possessed Samaria and lived in its cities."** As a result, the people there were mixed in race and with regard to religion - part Jewish, part pagan.

It is interesting to note that when Jesus refers to the "gift of God," she does not react at all in a negative way. I don't see in the subsequent conversation negative reactions, even when Jesus tells her **"...you worship what you do not know we worship what we do know (John 4:22."** What I see here is polite, serious discussion between the two. But when we come to verse 25 of John chapter 4, I see positive signals. When she says **"I know that Messiah is coming (He who is called Christ); when that One comes, He will declare all things to us (John 4:26)."** She is now ready to receive the ultimate truth: **"...I who speak to you am He** (John 4:26)."

SHE'S A CHILD OF GOD

When we read in verse 28 of John chapter 4, **"So the woman left her waterpot, and went into the city and said to the men, 'Come, see a man who told me all the things I have done; this is not the Christ, is it?"** This is a polite way of saying to these men, "Could this be the Christ?" She believes and makes a suggestion to the men of the city that she has found the Christ. More importantly, I think that Jesus knows that this Samaritan woman has become a child of God. This is indicated by the verses that follow.

HIS JOY

When the disciples arrive back at the well, they are surprised to find that He is not hungry, **"Meanwhile the disciples were urging Him, saying, 'Rabbi, eat' But He said to them, 'I have food to eat that you do not know about (John 4:31).'"** For me, this is a very special passage of Scripture. I don't know of any other passage like it, one that reveals to us the kind of joy that Jesus experiences here. It is the joy of realizing that a woman, one who has had a difficult and sad life, and one who is a Samaritan, considered to be unclean to the Jews, has now become a redeemed child of God. It was a very special and strange encounter, this appointment that His Father had ordained to take place at Jacob's well. Someone, it seems, had sown the seed in her heart and now Jesus is realizing the joy of reaping that soul for God.

HE IS NOT HUNGRY

He is a man in all respects, though also the Son of God. He is a man and He is not hungry. He tells the disciples that His food is to do the will of the Father. We read, **"...My food is to do the will of the will of Him who sent Me (John 4:34)."** I believe the He is rejoicing in what has been done in this woman's life. Her story has been a sad one. But now she has met the Messiah and in her joy she is spreading the news to others.

HE HAS BEEN ON A MISSION

He has been on a mission ordained by the Father. His Father had put this on His appointment calendar. Jesus has deliberately traveled into the hostile territory of Samaria. He has sent the disciples away to buy food so that He could have a private conversation with a woman in whom the seed has been sown. He begins by speaking with her about water. The end result is that a woman whose life has been very sad has now entered the kingdom of God. All of this had been planned by His Father. And now He is rejoicing in what the will of God has brought about. The joy of savoring that food leaves no room for a hunger for physical food.

SECTION TWO

APPOINTMENTS FUTURE

APPOINTMENTS FUTURE AND "THE HEART OF REVELATION"

In Section One we noted a number of God ordained appointments that have occurred in the past (as recorded in the book of Acts) and in the present. (I shared some of my experiences.) Needless to say, we can only look at God's appointment calendar after the fact. We can observe what God in His wisdom ordained and put in place as we look back on what He has done.

We will now consider the Final Appointment, Christ's meeting with planet earth at the time of His second coming and also that of individuals who come to Christ during that final period known as the Tribulation. In the book of Revelation, we can observe many of the details of that future time, but we cannot know when it will transpire. In verse 3 of Revelation chapter one we read, **"Blessed is he who reads and those who hear the words of the prophecy, and heed the things which are written in it; for the time is near."**

In a consideration of Revelation chapters 5 –10, I want to share with the reader what I have found to be a great blessing to me. I refer to those chapters as the "Heart of Revelation." I believe that the main story of the book is found set forth chronologically in those chapters (Revelation chapters 5-10).

We will also notice, in a survey of these scriptures, that even in that coming end time, God has set up appointments by which many come to Him. We will take note of the 144,000 Jewish people of Revelation chapter seven who follow the Lamb during those days. Looking ahead to chapter 14 of Revelation, verse 1, we read that they have **"His name and the name of His Father written on their foreheads."** And in verses 3-4 of Revelation chapter 14 we read, **"...And they sang a new song before the throne and before the four living creatures and the elders; and no one could learn the song except the one hundred and forty-four thousand who had been purchased from the earth...these are the ones who follow the Lamb wherever He goes. These have been purchased from among men as first fruits to God and to the Lamb."** We can only wonder about their individual stories of finding Jesus. They sing a new song that no one else can learn. We wonder as to how that comes about -- some day in that future day when God has placed people on His appointment calendar.

It is my thinking that the 144,000 Jews become the servants whom the Lord sends to many others who have begun to seek Him. Even during those future times of great trial our God is bringing people together. It's all on His appointment calendar.

CHAPTER EIGHT

THE MAIN STORY

Some years ago, a certain Bible teacher and pastor wrote the following story: "A man bought a farm with the signed agreement that he would take possession and move onto his property on April first of that year. Several months later when the time had come, he went to his new property to occupy and enjoy his new farm. However, the previous owner refused to leave. He wouldn't let the rightful new owner through the gate onto his property. Consequently, the rightful owner went back to town, obtained a copy of the deed and recruited the help of the sheriff and his deputies. When they arrived at the property the usurper decided to put up a fight. And it was a great fight. Windows were broken. The chicken house was burned down. Fences were torn down. It was a dramatic and awful scene until finally the usurper was subdued and finally hauled off to jail." (This is not an exact quotation, but the story as I remember it as told by Pastor R. I. Humberd in a commentary on the book of Revelation, written in 1944, now out of print.)

I suggest now to the reader that the above story is a simple paraphrase of the main story of the book of Revelation as it is told in Chapters 5-10 of that writing. Jesus obtains the titled deed (the scroll) from the hand of His Father. As soon as he proceeds to break the seals and open it the great struggle begins. Anti-Christ arrives on the scene and begins to conquer and occupy what rightfully belongs to the Son of God. There is death and destruction on the earth. But God's mighty hand of judgment falls. The seven trumpets are sounded and finally as the seven thunders of God's wrath are heard, Jesus takes possession of what He has purchased. Later on in the writing, in Rev. 20:10, we read that the evil usurper, the devil, is thrown into his own special jail, the lake of fire where he is "tormented day and night forever and ever."

The blessing that I realize in the story is the fact that my Savior, whom I love, who has redeemed me, as well as planet earth, takes possession of what is rightfully His. He will bring an end to the misery and evil that has held sway over the world which He created and then redeemed by the shedding of His own precious blood. It is a story of redemption.

CHAPTER NINE

A STORY OF REDEMPTION

Let me now call attention to the contextual relationship of chapters four and five of Revelation. At the end of chapter four we read of the great praise that is directed to God because He is the great creator. This praise emanates from "twenty-four elders" (Rev. 4: 10) and the four living creatures (Rev. 4:6-9). I do not want at this point to share all the reasons why I believe what I do about them now. I believe that the twenty-four elders represent God's people who have arrived in heaven. They come from the Twelve Tribes of Israel and from the church of Christ which is founded upon the twelve apostles. Twelve plus twelve equals twenty- four.

The 24 elders are dressed in white robes, sit on twenty-four thrones and have golden crowns on their heads. (Rev. 4:4.) The four living creatures refer to a special class of angels who are attached to the throne of God. Their description is like that of the angels found in Ezekiel chapters 1-10 (Cherubim) and Isaiah chapter 6 (Seraphim). I think that is enough said about them at this point, but notice what is said in the 11th and final verse of Rev. chapter four:

"Worthy are You, our Lord and our God, to receive glory and honor and power; for You created all things, and because of your will they existed, and were created." We notice that the word "<u>created</u>" occurs twice in Rev. 4:11. God is being praised because He is the creator.

In chapter 5 of Revelation the emphasis is upon redemption. Although the word redemption is not found, we have the word "purchased" in verse 9 of Rev. 5:

> **"And they sang a new song saying, 'Worthy are You to take the book and to break its seals for You were slain, and purchased to God with Your blood *men* from every tribe and tongue and people and nation." You have made them to *be* a kingdom of priests to our God; and they will reign upon the earth."'**
> [Emphasis mine]

We notice also that the congregation praising God is presented as being larger than what saw in Rev. chapter 4. Not only do we have the twenty-four elders and four living creatures, but we also have **"many angels...and the number of them was myriads of myriads, and thousands and thousands saying with a loud voice, 'Worthy is the Lamb that was slain to receive power and riches and wisdom and might and honor and glory and blessing (Rev. 5:11-12).'"**

The praise to the redeemer is thunderous and powerful beyond our imagination. We ask now the question, "Why this great joy? What is happening here that is so significant to the heavenly hosts?"

THE LITTLE BOAT TWICE OWNED

There is a story book written for children that I remember as being taught in Sunday School at a church where I pastored. It's the story about a little boy who, with his father, made out of wood a little boat that he could float on a near-by pond. The boy so much enjoyed that boat, floating it on the pond and pulling it in all directions by means of a string tied to it.

But then one day there was a commotion up on the street with the sounds of fire engines and much excitement. The boy pulled the little boat up on the land and ran to the street to see what was happening. After a while, when the excitement quieted, he went back down to the pond. But much to his dismay, his little boat was gone. "It couldn't have just floated away," he thought. After an hour or so of looking everywhere he went back home with great sadness in his heart.

Several months later the boy was walking on a sidewalk down-town when it caught his eye. In the window of a little shop, there was his boat. There was no mistake about it. It was his boat, the one he had made with the help of his father. Now it was for sale and the cost was quite high. The boy went home and retrieved some money that he had made on his paper route.

He went back to that shop and bought back the little boat that really belonged to him all along ["Little Book Twice Owned" by Mrs. Floyd McCague, Pub. Living Stories Inc. Jan. 1, 1966]. (That is a summary of the story as I recall it.) The boy redeemed that which he had created.

In that illustrated gospel book for children is the story of creation and redemption. It illustrates what we have presented in Revelation chapters 4 and 5. The scroll that we see in the Fathers hand in chapter 5 of Revelation verse 1 has to do with redemption. It's about the redemption of that which had been created.

JEREMIAH'S LAND DEAL

In the 32nd chapter of Jeremiah the prophet is instructed by the Lord to enter into a seemingly unwise land deal. He is told to buy a piece of land that for all intents and purposes was worthless. Here is the passage:

> "And Jeremiah said, 'The word of the Lord came to me, saying, "Behold, Hanamel the son of Shallum your uncle is coming to you, saying, 'Buy for yourself my field which is at Anathoth, for you have the right of redemption to buy it.' Then Hanamel my uncle's son came in to me in the court of the guard according to the word of the Lord and

said to me, 'Buy my field, please, that is at Anathoth, which is in the land of Benjamin; for you have the right of possession and the redemption is yours.' Then I knew that this was the word of the Lord (Jeremiah 32: 6-8)."

A prominent theme in the Old Testament is "the law of the kinsman redeemer" as set forth in the law of Moses. Simply put, if a man must sell a piece of property, the nearest relative has the right to buy it. It's a matter of keeping it in the family. This could also involve the widow of a man who had died, as we find illustrated in the story of Ruth as found in the book of Ruth. A near relative was obligated to offer to marry the widow.

The word for the redeemer is *goel*. In that story a man by the name of Boaz was the *goel*. He married Ruth. In Jeremiah chapter 32 it's a matter of the land.

In this case the land would seem to be worthless. For forty years the prophet has been warning the kings of Judah that the Babylonians were going to conquer and take over the land. In fact, they are now at the walls of the city and the land that Jeremiah's cousin wants to sell him is at Anathoth, which is already in the hands of the Babylonians. But Jeremiah goes ahead with the purchase because the Lord has spoken. He proceeds to undertake it all legally, having witnesses and (we assume) having it done in the presence of a judge.

Beginning in verse 9 of Jeremiah chapter 32 we read, "**I bought the field which was at Anathoth from Hanamel my** uncle's son, and I weighed out the silver for him, seventeen shekels of silver. I signed and sealed the deed, and called in witnesses, and weighed out the silver on the scales. Then I took the deeds of purchase, both the sealed *copy containing* the terms and conditions and the open copy and I gave the deed of purchase to Baruch the son of Neriah, the son of Mahseiah, in the sight of Hanamel my uncle's *son* and in the sight of witnesses who signed the deed of purchase, before all the Jews who were sitting in the court of the guard (Jeremiah 32: 9-12)"

We now notice a significant part of this story. Baruch is instructed to put the deed in what we might call the safety deposit box of the day. **"And I commanded Baruch in their presence saying, thus says the Lord of hosts, the God of Israel, 'Take these deeds, the sealed deed of purchase and this open deed, and put them in an earthenware jar, that they might last a long time (Jeremiah 32:13-14)."** In recent years archaeologists have discovered a number of earthen jars that were used for such a purpose—that is, for security

Why are there two deeds, the sealed one and the open one? The sealed copy was the official one, while the open deed indicated the contents as an easier point of reference. Later, in Roman times, just one sealed copy was involved. In verse 15 of Jeremiah 32 we have these significant words, **"For thus says the LORD of hosts, the God of Israel, 'Houses and fields and vineyards will again be bought in this land.'"** After the many years of being captive to Babylon, the land and its people will be restored. A descendant of Jeremiah would then be able to lay hold of the deed and occupy the property which Jeremiah has purchased as a kinsman redeemer.

All of this is presented to the reader to support the thought of redemption as found in Revelation chapter 5. The book in the hand of the Father (Rev. 5:1), I believe, is the title deed to planet earth. It has been safely kept in the safety of the Father's hand for many years. Now, the "Lion of the tribe of Judah," the Lamb of God will take the scroll and open the seals and proceed to take possession of that which was first created and then redeemed by His precious blood. Jesus is the kinsman redeemer, the *"goel."* The word translated "book" is *bibleon*. It refers to a scroll which has been rolled up with wax seals fastened to the edge. It has been rolled up and sealed seven times.

The wonderful joyous praise that we see as the Lamb takes the scroll to unroll it and begins to take possession of that which He has redeemed is in contrast to what Paul writes in Romans chapter eight:

> **"For I consider that the sufferings of this present time are not worthy to be compared with the glory that is to be revealed to us. For the anxious longing of the <u>creation </u>waits eagerly for the revealing of the sons of God. For the <u>creation</u> was subject to futility, not willingly, but because of Him who subjected**

it, in hope that the <u>creation</u> itself also will be set free from its slavery to corruption into the freedom of the glory of the children of God. For we know that the whole <u>creation</u> groans and suffers the pains of childbirth together until now. And not only this, but also, we ourselves, having the first fruits of the Spirit, even we ourselves groan within ourselves, waiting eagerly for our adoption as sons, the <u>redemption</u> of the body (Romans 8:18-23)." [Emphasis mine]

We read in these verses that creation "groans (Rom. 8:22)" and we "groan" (Rom. 8:23). waiting for the realization of redemption when Jesus comes to take control.

Why do we read of such thunderous praise? Why is there such joy on the part of the twenty-four elders, the four living creatures and myriads and myriads of angels? Is it because of the terrible things that are to happen on earth as the scroll is unrolled? Is there great joy because of the judgments that are about to fall on earth? Do we rejoice in a spirit of vengeance? I don't think so. I think it is the realization that the Lamb of God, the redeemer is about to take possession of that which belongs to Him.

ADDITIONAL NOTE ON THE KINDSMAN REDEEMER

"It was the responsibility of the kinsman redeemer in Jewish society to buy back the property of his nearest relative, or to redeem the relative himself from service to another, if the latter had previously sold his property or himself [as a slave]. The best known and most important example is that of Ruth and Boaz. Both Ruth and her mother-in-law were widowed and desired to have Boaz take the role of the kinsman redeemer, which resulted in his marrying Ruth." [From the New American Standard Bible Dictionary, p 79.]

CHAPTER TEN

FINAL RESISTANCE

Remember now the story we told previously of the man who bought a farm and with title deed in hand went to occupy that which he had purchased. The usurper refused to leave and there ensued a violent battle. Such is the case that we read of in Rev. 6:2, even though God in His sovereignty is controlling the action. A white-horse rider, the Anti-Christ, rides onto the scene "…conquering and going out to conquer…." John Walvoord in his commentary on the book of Revelation, states that he does not believe that the white horse rider here is Jesus Christ. This is not the same as Christ coming on a white horse as found in Rev.19:11. He says,

> "A more plausible explanation is that the rider of this white horse is none other than 'the prince that shall come' of Daniel 9:26, who is to head up the revived Roman Empire and ultimately becomes the world ruler." [John Walvoord, p. 126]. Jennings states, "The whole

content and character of these seals absolutely forbid our thinking of this rider being the Lord Jesus, as so many affirm. His reign shall not bring war, famine, and strife in its train." [F.A. *Jennings*, p. 201].

And that is what we have with the first four seals of Rev. chapter 6. They represent war, famine and death. Authority was given to him to bring death upon a quarter of the world. We read, "**...Authority was given to them over a fourth of the earth, to kill with sword and with famine and with pestilence and by the wild beasts of the earth (Rev. 6:8).**" The wide spread death mentioned here is very difficult to fathom. It speaks of how terrible this period of time is going to be.

CHAPTER ELEVEN

THE CRY OF THE MARTYRED

The Fifth Seal – Revelation 6:9-11

"When the Lamb broke the fifth seal, I saw underneath the altar the souls of those who had been slain because of the word of God, and because of the testimony which they had maintained; and they cried out with a loud voice saying 'How long, O Lord holy and true, will You refrain from judging and avenging our blood on those who dwell on the earth (Rev. 6:9-10)?'"

So, there will be some of God's people on earth during this time of great tribulation. Now we see the souls of some who are now in Heaven, having been martyred for Christ. We read here of their souls, not their bodies. In chapter 20 of the book of Revelation, we read of the resurrection of "**... those who**

**had been beheaded because of their testimony of Jesus
and because of the word of God, and those who had not
worshipped the beast or his image, and had not received the
mark on their forehead and on their hand; ... (Rev. 20:4)."**

But here in chapter 6, verses 9-11 we read of their souls, as
they wait for the completion of God's plan for them.

I have often wondered about this, the fifth seal, as to how
it fits in with the other seals presented in Revelation chapter
six. I believe that the other seals speak of God's judgment on
this world. But on the surface, this would seem to be different.
Now I see that although the cries of the martyred would seem
not to be a seal of judgment, it does fit in because what we have
now is the people of God crying out for more judgment. As
commentator Robert Thomas points out, "...these prayers serve
to make a dismal future even more frightening because of the
intercession of those especially precious in God's sight (Robert
Thomas, p. 44 1)." We point out that the sixth seal is especially
severe, with major earthquakes taking place and **"mountains
and islands moved out of their places** (Rev. 6:14), and men
saying to the mountains and to the rocks, **'Fall on us and hide
us from the presence of Him who sits on the throne, and
from the wrath of the Lamb, for the great day of their wrath
has come, and who is able to stand (Rev. 6:15,16).'"** Perhaps
this is in response to the cries of the martyred.

SEVERAL POINTS

First, there will be followers of Christ on earth during this period of tribulation. We will get into this more in our consideration of Revelation chapter seven. But as Walvoord points out "...it will be difficult to declare one's faith in the Lord Jesus. It may very well be that the majority of those who trust in Christ as Savior in that day will be put to death (Walvoord, p. 134)."

Secondly, the enemy is fighting back. They can't very well fight against God, so they are fighting against His people on earth. There is a verse in I John that is important in this regard. We read, "**We know that we are of God, and the whole world lies in the power of the evil one (I John 5:19).**" It can be translated this way, "**The whole world lies in the lap of the evil one.**" He is in control of the kosmos (the world). The kosmos in I John is the world system. He has his people -- the Anti-Christ (who is the beast of chapter 13), the False prophet, and the kings of this world. The method of warfare during this seven-year period is to kill anyone who will not receive the mark of the Beast (Rev. 13:17).

Thirdly, we read that the souls of the martyrs are beneath the altar. I agree with the commentators who say that this is not the altar of burnt offering that we read of in the Old Testament, but the altar of sweet incense that is also a part of the Tabernacle set-up. A sweet incense going up from that altar represents the prayers of God's people to Him. They are praying, **"How long, O Lord, holy and true, will You refrain from judging and avenging our blood on those who dwell on the earth (Rev. 6:10)?"** Their prayers are sweet to Him. These people are precious in His sight.

We notice now they prayed: They do not pray, **"Father, forgive them for they know not what they do (Luke 23:34):** Thomas in his commentary on the book of Revelation puts it this way, "…these martyrs are now beyond their mortal state and are not subject to its limitations (Thomas, p. 447). He says also that "a prayer for pardon is more appropriate for a time of grace."

Fourthly, we notice also that they are referred to as souls. The Greek word here is psychas, from which we get the word psychiatry. Thomas says the word "…refers to the total person as a rational being (p.443)." He goes on, "John saw only the souls, because their bodies had not yet been resurrected (cf. Rev. 20:4)."

Finally, we read that God tells them to rest a while longer, **"…and they were told to rest for a little while longer, until the number of their fellow servants and their brethren who were to be killed even as they had been, would be completed also (Rev. 6:11)."**

Now we ask a question which is in accordance with our argument in this writing. How did these martyrs come to know Christ? Did our God bring people together so as to bring the seeker into contact with a servant of God? In chapter seven of Revelation, we will take note of the 144,000 Jews who come to Christ, probably in some special way. I am inclined to believe that the 144,000, become the evangelists, the missionaries to the lost in those very troublesome times. Perhaps, some day we will know their stories. And what exciting stories they will be! And these divine appointments will take place after the church has been raptured into Heaven.

It is not my intention to interpret and explain all the details of the seals, trumpets, etc., set forth in these chapters. I want rather to present an overview of these chapters in order to convey the main story of the book as found in chapters 5 through 10 of the Book of Revelation.

CHAPTER TWELVE

SEVENS WILD

I am not referring to the game of poker but to the plenitude of sevens in the book of Revelation. There are seven churches, seven spirits, seven golden lampstands, seven stars, etc. In Vine's Dictionary of Old and New Testament Words, [p. 1025], he writes, "The word is sometimes used as an expression of fulness…It generally expresses completeness and it is used most frequently in the Apocalypse." In these chapters we have before us three series of seven. There are seven seals, seven trumpets and seven thunders. The seven <u>bowls</u> of God's wrath are found in the second half of the book. In verse 11 of Rev. chapter 10 we have these words:

"And they said to me, 'You must prophesy again concerning many peoples and nations and tongues and kings (Rev. 10:11)." I believe that the main story of the book of Revelation is found in chapters 5-10. Beginning in chapter eleven of Revelation we have a more detailed account of many aspects of the tribulation period. It's in this second half of the book that we read of the seven vials or bowls of God's wrath.

There is much food for thought as to the meaning of those seven vials of God's wrath. I will not go into that here. We now look at the format of the three series of sevens as found in these chapters (Rev. 5-10). Notice that the seven trumpets are contained in the seventh seal. The seven thunders occur as the seventh trumpet is about to sound. Please find below a diagram that endeavors to depict the layout of the seals, trumpets and thunders as set forth in chapters six through ten of Revelation. The thunders are not explained, but just set forth as a culmination of God's judgment upon a rebellious world.

It looks like this:

SEALS

1 2 3 4 5 6 (:) 7

TRUMPETS

1 2 3 4 5 6 (:::) 7

THUNDERS

The seven trumpets are included in and make up the seventh seal. Notice also that after the announcement of the 6th seal and before the opening of the 7th seal there is an interlude or a pause in the action This is indicated by the sign of a parenthesis I have included in the diagram. The same is true concerning the trumpets. After the 6th trumpet and before we get to the 7th, there is an interlude, or pause before the 7th trumpet is blown. Furthermore, the interlude section in chapter 7 has two parts while in the interlude in chapter 10 is much longer having several parts, actually extending into chapter 11. The seven thunders mentioned in chapter 10 predict what will happen when the seventh trumpet sounds (Rev. 11:115,16)

Again, I will not try to interpret the meaning of all of the details of these chapters concerning the seals and trumpets. I will let others decide what is meant by, for example, "...**a great mountain burning fire was thrown into the sea, and a third of the sea became blood (Rev. 8:8).**" I do have thoughts concerning what is symbol and what is literal concerning many of these verses, but I am not inclined to share them here. It is beyond my purpose in this writing to do so. Rather, strange as it may seem to the reader at this point, I want to devote a lot of thought to the interlude sections, that which is between the 6th and 7th seal and what is between the 6th and 7th trumpet. Between the 6th and 7th seal we learn about the 144,000 Jews who are living during this period and of the great multitude who arrive in Heaven "**having washed their robes in the blood of the Lamb (Rev. 7:14)**".

CHAPTER THIRTEEN

144,000 SPECIAL PEOPLE

Revelation chapter seven.

They are Jews. I know that because that it is what it says. In Rev. 7:4 we read, **"And I heard the number of those who were sealed from every tribe of the sons of Israel."** Furthermore, beginning in verse 5 of Rev. chapter 7, there are names given for the twelve tribes of Israel. In God's eyes there are no lost tribes of Israel. It is true that the names listed are a little different than they are in other places scripture. The tribe of Dan is omitted for some reason, perhaps because they were the first tribe to fall into the idolatry of the surrounding nations. The first-born son of Joseph is listed, (Manasseh) along with Joseph. But that does not really matter. When we read of Judah, Benjamin, Asher, Levi, etc., we know that we are reading of the sons of Jacob.

NOT ALLEGORY OR SYMBOLISM

I find it difficult to believe, as some do, that these many names somehow refer to the church of Christ or to some special group within Christendom. It is true that in the book of Revelation it is sometimes difficult to determine whether something is literal or figurative. When some reference is figurative, it is usually easy to spot. For example, in Rev. 19:15, concerning the second coming of Christ we read, **"From His mouth comes a sharp sword, so that with it He may strike down the nations, and He will rule them with a rod of iron: ..."** I find it hard to visualize Jesus coming with a sword coming out of His mouth. But I remember that in Hebrews 4:12 we read, **"For the word of God is living and active and sharper than any two- edged sword...."** But perhaps more important is the fact that in the creation story of Genesis, as found in chapters one and two, we have the repeated saying, as in Genesis 1:3, **"And the Lord said, 'Let there be light;' and there was light."** The phrase, **"And God said"** is repeated over and over again referring to the creative power of the word of "God. We read in Hebrews 1:3 that He "...**upholds all things by the word of His power...**" In chapter 11 of Hebrews, verse 3 we read, **"By faith we understand the worlds were prepared by the word of God...,"** So the symbolism is not hard to understand. At His second coming He will direct the power of His word to judgment upon his enemies.

Another example can be found in the vision of a **"woman**

who is clothed with the sun, and the moon under her feet, and on her head a crown of twelve stars... (Rev. 12:1)." Again, common sense causes us to believe that this is not literal. So, what is the point of reference in the Old Testament? In Genesis chapter 37, verse 9 we read that Joseph, one of the sons of Jacob, had a dream. We read, **"Now he had still another dream, and related it to his brothers, and said 'Lo, I have had another dream; and behold, the sun and moon and eleven stars were bowing down to me.'"** Then in Gen. 37:10 we see that his father, Jacob knew exactly what his son was saying, **"...What is this dream that you have had? Shall I and your mother and your brothers actually come to bow ourselves down before you to the ground?'"** From this passage we have good reason to believe that the symbolism of Rev. 12:1 refers to the nation Israel; which nation was developed from the twelve sons of Jacob (Israel), which nation is being persecuted by the devil during the tribulation period.

But what about the 144,000 spoken of in Rev. 7:4? What could possibly be a point of reference for not only speaking of the fact that they are sons of Israel, but for listing all the tribes as consisting of twelve each? It might be one thing to believe in replacement theology, that Israel has forfeited all the promises made to them because of their rejection of Christ and that therefore the church of Christ has replaced them as being the recipient of the promises. But how do you find meaning in listing the twelve individually? Does the church of Christ somehow consist of twelve tribes? I don't see how you can find anything in the Old Testament to justify that. It is much easier to just take the passage in a literal sense. This is a reference to Jewish people who have a place in God's program in the end times.

EIGHT THINGS ABOUT THE 144 THOUSAND

1. <u>As stated above, they are Jews</u>,
2. <u>They are sealed</u> before the seven trumpets are sounded. They are protected from the winds of God's judgments as set forth in the blowing of the trumpets. We read of this in verses 1-3 of Rev. chapter 7.

(We now move to the 14th chapter of Revelation, verses 1-5 where we find more details about these special people.)

3. <u>They are with the Lamb on Mt. Zion.</u> This seems to look forward to the beginning of the coming kingdom of Christ on earth (1000 years).
4. <u>They have the name of the Lamb and the name of His Father</u> written on their foreheads. The seal that they received on their foreheads is not just a seal of protection, but a seal of ownership. They have come to know Jesus.
5. <u>They have a new song to sing</u>. We find them here involved in the unimaginable sound of a huge choir. We read that they sing "**a new song** (Rev. 14:3)." What does it mean to sing a new song? We find that terminology in

Psalm 96:1, Psalm 98:1 and Psalm 144:9. In those verses we are encouraged to sing a new song. We read, "**Sing to the Lord a new song; Sing to the Lord all the earth. Sing to the Lord, bless His name; Proclaim good tidings of His salvation from day to day (Ps. 9:1-2)** and "**O sing to the Lord a new song, For He has done wonderful things (Ps.98:1).** In Ps. 144:9,10 the psalmist says, "**I will sing a new song to You, O God; Upon a harp of ten strings. I will sing praises to you, Who gives salvation to kings...**" What does it mean to sing "a new song?"

Merrill Unger in his commentary on the Old Testament, volume 1, page 888 says the following:

> "This is a millennial psalm...the first of five singing Psalms (96-100) that celebrate the King's reign when the ransomed of the LORD shall return, and come to Zion with songs and everlasting "joy (Psalm 96:12)." That would seem to fit the circumstance of the 144,000 Jews here. They have come through the tribulation and could very well sing Psalm 96. Unger goes on to say, "The song is styled a new song (Ps.40:3) because it celebrates <u>a new</u> <u>blessing</u> never experienced before, namely, the

redemptive work as it affects the subjects of the millennial kingdom and those who in that age will 'reign on the earth (Rev. 5:9-10)." [Unger page 888]

What about your spiritual experience? Can you say with the Psalmist as found in Ps. 4:3, **"He put a new song in my mouth, a song of praise to God; Many will see and fear and will trust in the Lord."** I believe that it refers to the realization of some new blessing in one's life. That is to say, "a new and good blessing has come to me in my life, and I will sing about it."

Now the question is: What is the new blessing about which the 144,000 sing?

6. <u>They have a song to sing that no one else can learn</u>. **"And no one could learn the song except the 144,000 (Rev. 14:3)."** That is to say, I believe, that they have had a unique experience about which they can now sing. Was it the manner in which God protected them during those tribulation years, or was it the manner in which they came to Christ in the first place? If you believe, as I do, that the rapture of the church has already taken place and all of God's people have been removed from the earth, how then would they be led to Christ? Was it a dramatic and special conversion such as Paul experienced on the road to Damascus? Nevertheless, they have a song to sing that no one

else can sing. The have had a blessing that is exclusive to them. What kind of an appointment did the Lord ordain for each one of them? The text seems to imply that it was exclusively theirs and we can perhaps surmise that it was different for each one of them. Perhaps we can ask them someday.

7. They have been redeemed to God as "**first fruits to God and the Lamb** (Rev. 14:4)." When, in the Fall of the year, you go to an orchard and pick a few apples that are red and ready to be picked, we could say that those few apples are the first fruits of the great harvest of apples to come. So, these 144,00 children of Israel are the first fruits of what great harvest? Are they the first ones to come to Christ during those terrible days, or are they the first of the Jewish people who will trust in their Messiah during those days?

8. They "**follow the Lamb wherever He goes** (Rev. 14:4)," and in doing so we read that **"They have not been defiled with women, for they have kept themselves chaste...and no lie was found in their mouth (Rev. 14:4,5)."** Does this speak of chaste behavior in the literal sense, or does it refer to keeping oneself pure from spiritual fornication with the great harlot of Rev. 17:1? I will let the reader decide. Perhaps both are involved.

FUTURE PLANS FOR ISRAEL

Let us now come back to the matter of God's plan for Israel. In Romans chapter 11 the apostle Paul has much to say about the chosen people of God. In his illustration of the Olive Tree, he states that the nation Israel someday will once again be grafted into the place of blessing that the Olive Tree represents, "...**how much more will these who are the natural branches be grafted into their own olive tree? For I do not want you, brethren, to be uninformed of this great mystery---so that you will not be wise in your own estimation ---that a partial hardening has happened to Israel until the fulness of the Gentiles has come in; and so, all Israel will be saved; just as it is written, 'The DELIVERER WILL COME FROM ZION, HE WILL REMOVE UNGODLINESS FROM JACOB. THIS IS MY COVENANT WITH THEM WHEN I TAKE AWAY THEIR SINS (Romans 11:24-27).'"** (I invite the reader to study further all of Paul's teaching here with regard to His illustration of the Olive Tree as found in Romans chapter 11.) I find it very exciting to think of the 144,000 people of Israel as being the first fruits of a great harvest of the Jewish people during the End Times.

ISRAEL'S SPIRIITUAL DELIVERANCE ACCORDING TO ZECHARIAH

Let me now share the very powerful and wonderful prophecy concerning the nation Israel as written by the prophet Zechariah. He speaks of a "divinely provided fountain of cleansing" in Zech. 13:1 [Duane Lindsey in the Bible Knowledge Commentary, P. 1567]

"In that day a fountain will be opened for the house of David and for the inhabitants of Jerusalem, for sin and impurity (Zech.13:1)." In chapter 12 of Zechariah, we read of an outpouring of the Holy Spirit and the mourning of Israel. "The Israelites will receive enablement to '**look on Me, the One they have pierced (Zech. 12:10)** [a term usually indicating piercing to death. [Linsey, p. 1567] "'The piercing' evidently refers to the rejection of Christ (as God incarnate) and crucifying, though the word does not specifically refer to crucifixion." [Duane Lindsay, p.1567] The passage goes on to speak of a great national mourning on part of the Jews on that future day:

> **"I will pour out on the house of David and on the inhabitants of Jerusalem, the Spirit of grace and of supplication, so that they will look upon Me whom they have pierced; and they will mourn for Him, as one mourns for an only son, and they will weep bitterly over Him like the bitter weeping over a**

firstborn. In that day there will be great mourning in Jerusalem, like the mourning of Hadadrimmon in the plain of Megiddo. The land will mourn, every family by itself; the family of the house of David by itself and their wives by themselves...all the families that remain, every family by itself and their wives by themselves (Zech. 12:10-14)."

The Scripture speaks of a great future for the nation Israel which begins when they turn at last to Jesus as their Messiah. The 144,000 of Rev. chapters 7 and 14 are plainly Jews. They have the name of the Lamb written on their foreheads and the name of His Father as well. They come to God in great numbers, the 144,000 being the "first fruits."

144,000 APPOINTMENTS

They are on God's appointment calendar. At some point in the future each of them has an appointment to meet with the Lord. It is difficult to imagine just how this will take place. Will God use someone to meet with them? Or will he meet with them in some special way? Will each of them be seeking to know Him before the appointment takes place? Perhaps someday their stories will be told. As I said, "perhaps we can ask them."

CHAPTER FOURTEEN

THE OTHER GREAT MULTIITUDE

We will now consider more of the contents of the interlude that occurs between the opening of the six and seventh Seals as found in Revelation chapter seven. We read now about another great multitude involved in the days of the tribulation period:

> **"After these things I looked, and behold, a great multitude which no one could count, from every nation and _all_ tribes and peoples and tongues, standing before the throne and before the Lamb, clothed in white robes, and palm branches were in their hands (Rev. 7:9)."**

There are some who suggest that the two multitudes of people set forth in Rev. chapter seven are one and the same. But the plain language seems to say otherwise. In contrast to a listing of the twelve tribes of Israel we now read of a **"great multitude...from <u>every nation</u> and _all_ tribes ... (Rev. 7:9)"** [emphasis mine]. So, there is presented to us a contrast between the twelve tribes of one nation and a multitude from every nation and tribe. How could the language be any plainer?

It seems that John is now directing our attention towards the end of the great tribulation period and the people who are coming out of the trials of that period, having come to follow Christ. We read that they **"have washed their robes and made them white in the blood of the Lamb** (Rev. 7:14)."

NOT THE RAPTURE

There are some who say that the words of Rev. 7:14 are a reference to the Rapture of the Church. Rather, as Robert L. Thomas states "We have in verse 14 of Rev. chapter 7 a present tense participle in the original Greek and thus reads, 'These are those who are coming out from the Great Tribulation...' ...The usual force of the present tense is to portray continuous action. The Semitic-style construction of the statement favors allowing this sense here." [Robert L. Thomas, *p.*495.] But the rapture as presented by the apostle Paul in I Corinthians chapter 15 and II Thess. chapter 4 happens at a point of time; **"For the Lord Himself will descend from heaven with a shout, with the voice of the archangel and with the trumpet of God, and the dead in Christ will rise first. (II Thess. 4:16)."** The rapture, our taking up suddenly to be with Him, takes places in a moment of time, as opposed to "...**those who are coming out of the great tribulation...**(Rev. 7:14)." In Corinthians 15

Paul speaks of the rapture and resurrection of God's people as happening **"in a moment, in the twinkling of an eye, …** (I Cor.15:52)."** The key to making this distinction is that the participle in Rev. 7:14 is in the present tense and speaks of continuous action. These people have been coming out of the Great Tribulation, having believed in Christ and then having suffered as martyrs for Him.

FOOD FOR THOUGHT

In Revelation chapter seven we have presented to us two great multitudes of people, people who come to Christ during the tribulation period. Is there a cause-and- effect relationship between the two? Do we have 144,000 missionaries who turn to God in some unusual way and then become those who turn many others to Him during this time, both Jews and Gentiles? Notice, that when the latter multitude arrives before the throne of God, the twenty-four elders (who represent the Church of Christ) are already there.

THE RAPTURE IN THE BOOK OF REVELATION?

It may seem strange but the Rapture of the church does not seem to be mentioned explicitly anywhere in the book. I cannot find a description like that of Paul in I Thess. chapter 4 anywhere in the book of Revelation. But I believe we do have an implicit reference to it in chapter 4 of the book of Revelation. It has to do with the "open door." We read there, **"After these things, I looked, and behold, a door standing open in heaven, and the first voice that I heard, like the sound of a trumpet speaking with me, said, 'Come up here, and I will show you what must take place after these things (Rev.4:1)"**

In chapters two and three of Revelation we read of the churches, but beginning in chapter four we read no more of the churches or the church of Jesus Christ in the book. Rather, we see in heaven from now on the twenty-four elders, who are dressed in white robes and who in verse 10 of Rev. chapter 4 **"cast their crowns before the throne."** They have been rewarded for their service to Christ and now worship their Lord along with the angels in Heaven. So, I believe the rapture is set forth implicitly in that phrase, **"a door standing open** (Rev. 4:1)." They have passed through that door which is still standing open. There is also the sound of a trumpet. John heard a voice, **"like the sound of a trumpet** (Rev. 4:1)." This would seem to connect with the passages that speak of the rapture. In I Corinthians 15:51 the word **"trumpet"** occurs twice. In First Thessalonians 4:16 Paul makes mention of the voice of the **"archangel"** and **"trumpet of God."** If the Revelation 4:1 passage is simply that of inviting John up to Heaven, why is that invitation given with the sound of a trumpet? Rather, I believe the Rapture of the Church is implied in that verse (Rev. 4:1). The Church of Christ is now in Heaven and we read no more of the "church" or "churches" in the chapters that follow, but wonderfully, God still has a plan for Israel and for those Gentles whom they will bless.

THE SEVEN TRUMPETS

It seems to me that the book of Revelation gives us the final exam of Bible study. How well one is able to determine the meaning of some vision or terminology found in Revelation depends upon how well one can remember and understand something that is set forth in the Old Testament. This is a case in point. When we read of "seven trumpets," does that ring a bell? Where else do we read of the blowing of seven trumpets? It's not hard to remember. It's famous. It's the story of Joshua and the battle of Jericho. This is what the Lord said to Joshua as found in the book of Joshua, chapter 6, verses 3-5:

> **"You shall march around the city, all the men of war circling the city once. You shall do it for six days. Also, seven priests shall carry seven trumpets of ram's horns before the ark; then on the seventh day you shall march around the city seven times, and the priests shall blow the trumpets. It shall be when they**

make a long blast with the ram's horn, and when you hear the sound of the trumpet, all the people shall shout with a great shout; and the wall of the city will fall down flat, and the people will go up every man straight ahead."

Notice that in that story there is seven within a seven. They march around the city for six days. And on the seventh day they march around the city seven times and blow the trumpets seven times. The grand conclusion comes on the seventh day. When the trumpets sound for the seventh time on that day, the walls of Jericho fall flat.

Likewise, here in these chapters of the book of Revelation, the seven trumpets sound as a part of the seventh seal—seven within a seven. Another interesting fact is that the Old Testament name "Joshua" is equivalent to the New Testament "Jesus." They really are the same name, one in the Hebrew of the Old Testament and one in the Greek of the New.

I don't believe this is coincidental. This is typology. The historical event known as The Battle of Jericho is a type that looks forward to the Second Coming when Jesus will conquer the world powers of planet earth. Make no mistake. The story of Jericho refers to an actual historical event. They really did blow those trumpets seven times, but it is also typology. It looks forward to that which we read of in the book of Revelation.

THE SEVEN TRUMPET JUDGMENTS

They are severe beyond our imagination. **"Then the angel took the censer and filled it with fire off the altar, and threw it to the earth; and there followed peals of thunder and sounds and flashes of lightning and an earthquake. ...The first angel sounded, and there came hail and fire, mixed with blood, and they were thrown to the earth; and a third of the earth was burned up, and a third of the trees were burned up, and all the green grass was burned up (Rev. 8:5,7)."**

These words are difficult to interpret. How much of this is symbolic as opposed to literal? I have some thoughts about it but I don't want to take the time and space to share them now. I think I know something of the meaning of it all, but I am not sure and do not want to get into it at this point. Looking ahead to the sounding of the fifth trumpet, we find something very terrible and very evil. Locusts and scorpions come out of a bottomless pit. Their purpose is to torture and torment the men who do not have the seal of God on their foreheads. Without getting into this passage too deeply it seems to me that we have here a picture of fierce demonic activity. We bear in mind what Jesus said about this period in Matthew 24:21, **"For then shall be a great tribulation, such as has not occurred since the beginning of the world until now, nor ever will."**

When we come to the blowing of the sixth trumpet, as

found in Rev. chapter 9, we seem to come to the great climax of the evil that comes upon the world at this time.

"And the four angels, who had been prepared for the hour and day and month and year, were released, so that they would kill a third of mankind. The number of the armies was two hundred million; I heard the number of them (Rev. 9:15,16)." It looks like demonic powers are being unleashed to inspire unprecedented warfare among men. I wonder if that is not always the case. Men go to war under Satanic influence. This is not to dismiss the evil that comes from the hearts of men.

The description of the weapons used looks a little like nuclear powered weapons; **"And this is how I saw in the vision the horses and those who sat on them:** *the riders* **had breastplates** *the color* **of fire and of hyacinth and of brimstone; and the heads of the horses are like the heads of lions; and out of their mouths proceed fire and smoke and brimstone (Rev. 9:17)."** These are not ordinary horses. I don't believe John in his day could find words to accurately describe what he saw. He has to use metaphor. Verse 19 of Rev. chapter 9 is interesting, **"For the power of the horses is in their mouths and in their tails; for their tails are like serpents and have heads and with them they do harm."** They look like modern day missiles. The power to propel is in the tail, while the deadly nuclear bomb is in the head. I have tried to summarize just a little of what is in these chapters.

CHAPTER SIXTEEN

THE ANGEL OF THE LORD

THE LITTLE BOOK

We come now to the interlude or pause in action that occurs between the sixth and seventh trumpet. We are looking at the first part of Revelation chapter 10. In the first part of that interlude, we are informed of something extremely important. It's about a strong angel who has in his hand, "**a little book, one which is open** (Rev. 10:1,2)." We bear in mind that we are considering a scroll, made out of parchment, or similar material. I believe that this is a reference to the same scroll that the Lamb of God receives out of the Father's hand as seen in chapter five of Revelation. But now it is described as little because the seals have been broken and the scroll is almost all unrolled, that is to say we are almost at the end of the process whereby Jesus takes possession of that which is rightfully His.

THE STRONG ANGEL

"**I saw another strong angel coming down out of heaven, clothed with a cloud; and the rainbow was upon his head, and his face was like the sun, and his feet like pillars of fire (Rev. 10:1).**" I have in mind several reasons for believing that this is none other than Jesus Christ Himself. First of all, the description of Him is very similar to the description that we find in chapter one of Revelation where it is clear that it is that of Christ. There it is said that "**His head and His hair were white like white wool, like snow and His eyes were like a flame of fire. His feet were like burnished bronze, when it has been made to glow in a furnace...His face was like the sun shining in its strength (Rev, 1:14-16).**" The angel pictured in Rev. 10:1 is also presented as having a "**face ...like the sun, and his feet like pillars of fire.**" He is also described as "**coming down out of heaven, clothed with a cloud; and the rainbow was upon His head (Rev. 10:1).**" This is certainly a picture of great majesty. Secondly, we read that a little book is in His hand. The last time we read of a book, or scroll, it was in the hand of the Lamb of God as it was received from the Father's hand. He has been breaking the seals. He has been unrolling the scroll.

THE ANGEL OF THE LORD

My third reason for believing that this is Christ Himself as described in verse one of Rev. chapter 10, has to do with the Old Testament references to the "Angel of the Lord." That exact terminology is found in the Old Testament but not in the New. The word "angel" means messenger. But there is one "Messenger" that is different than a Gabriel or Michael or any of the Seraphim or Cherubim. It is a remarkable and wonderful truth that the Son of God appears to men and women of the Old Testament in what many theologians call "theophanies." There are several accounts of this in the Old Testament record. I want to devote some space to this because many believers in Christ are unaware of it.

THE BURNING BUSH

We have a clear example of this in the account of Moses and the Burning Bush:

"The angel of the Lord appeared to Him in a blazing fire from the midst of the bush. ...when the Lord saw that he turned aside to look, God called to him from the midst of the bush and said, 'Moses, Moses! (Exodus 3:2,4).' Then He said, 'Do not come near here; remove your sandals from your feet, for the place on which you are standing is holy ground.' He said also, 'I am the God of your father, the God of Abraham, the God of Isaac, and the God of Jacob.' Then Moses hid his face, for he was afraid to look at God (Exodus 5:5,6)." Later in the chapter we read,

"God said to Moses, 'I am WHO I AM. Thus, you shall say to the sons of Israel, I AM has sent me to you

(Ex. 3:14).'" Read these verses carefully and you will realize that the one who is referred to as the Angel of the LORD in Ex. 3:2 is the same as the great I AM in Exodus 3:14. This is a Theophany, a manifestation of God in visible form.

THE THREE MEN AT ABRAHAM'S TENT

An earlier Theophany is found in Genesis chapter 18. It is important to notice the very first verse of Genesis chapter 18, **"Now the LORD appeared to him by the oaks of Mamre, while he was sitting at the tent door in the heat of the day."** The chapter then goes on to describe just how the LORD appeared to him. **"When he lifted up his eyes and looked, behold three men were standing opposite him; and when he saw them, he ran from the tent door to meet them and bowed himself to the earth, and said, 'My Lord, if now I have found favor in Your sight, please do not pass Your servant by (Gen 18:2,3)."**

In verse 10 of Gen. chapter 18 we read that one of the three makes an announcement concerning Sarah. Notice that the first-person pronoun is used, **"...I will surely return to you at this time next year; and behold, Sarah your wife will have a son. ..."** When we get down to verse 13 of Gen. chapter 18 the identity of one of the three becomes plain. The reader may remember that when the announcement is made that Sarah will have a child in her advanced old age, she laughs. And so, we read, **"And the LORD said to Abraham, 'Why did Sarah** laugh, saying, 'Shall I indeed bear a child when I am so old?'" (Gen. 18:13)."

The significant thing here is that we read at the beginning of Gen.18:13, "**And the LORD said...**" The word rendered LORD is the Hebrew word YAWEH. YAWEH is speaking to Abraham. Again, in verse 17 of Gen. chapter 18, "**And the LORD said, 'shall I hide from Abraham the thing that I do?'**" Then follows the extended dialogue between Abraham and the Lord concerning the fate of the city of Sodom.

We read in 22 of Gen. chapter 18 that the men turned away and went toward Sodom. We find out in verse 1 of Gen. chapter 19 that these two men were angels, "**Now the two angels came to Sodom in the evening as Lot was sitting in the gate of Sodom.**" Their task was to rescue Lot and his family from the city of Sodom which is to be destroyed. They went down into Sodom while the LORD is discussing the fate of the city with Abraham. As chapter 18 of Genesis begins, we read of three men who came to the tent of Abraham. It turns out that two of them were angels and the other was the LORD himself (Yahweh) appearing to Abraham in a theophany. (a physical manifestation of God). Many evangelical scholars believe that it is the second person of the trinity who appears in these theophanies. We'll look at that matter later on in our consideration.

THE MOTHER OF SAMSON

We are told in Judges 13:2 that the wife of Manoah was barren. We read in verse 3 of Judges chapter 13, **"Then the angel of the LORD appeared to the woman and said to her, 'Behold now, you are barren and have borne no children, but you shall conceive and give birth to a son.'"** What follows is a wonderful, extended account telling us of the Lord's message to the parents of Samson. The story extends from verse 2 of Judges chapter 13 to verse 24 of Judges chapter 13.

The Angel of the Lord first appeared to the wife of Manoah with the promise of a child and after that to the man and his wife together. The theophany ends dramatically in verse 22 with Manoah afraid for his life because as he says, **"We shall surely die, for we have seen God. But his wife says 'if the LORD (YAHWEH) had desired to kill us, He would not have accepted a burnt offering and a grain offering from our hands, nor would He have shown us all these things, nor would He have let us hear *things* like this at this time (Judges 13:22-23).'"**

I urge the reader to read all of Judges chapter 13. It is an interesting story in which the term, "Angel of the Lord," occurs ten times. Twice the visitor is called "Angel of God," four times "man of God," "man," three times, "God," once and "LORD" one time.

At one point in the story Manoah said to the Angel of the Lord, **"What is your name, so that when your words** come to pass, we may honor you? But the angel of the Lord said to him, 'Why do you ask my name, seeing it is wonderful (Judges 13:17)?'" Merrill F. Unger, on page 333 of his commentary says that the word translated "wonderful" means "incommunicable," or "ineffable." That is to say, "beyond human capacity to understand."

The last few words of Judges 13:21 compared to verse 22 of Judges chapter 13 are significant. **"... Then Manoah knew that he was the angel of the Lord. So, Manoah said to his wife, 'We will surely die, for we have seen God. (Judges 13:21,22).'"** For me, this passage is the most convincing of all. The term, "Angel of the Lord" does not refer merely to an angel, or some kind of a strong angel. It refers to an appearance of the Son of God in Old Testament history.

THE SECOND PERSON OF THE TRINITIY

You may be asking, "Why do you say that this manifestation of the divine involves the Second Person of the Trinity? Some theologians tie the scriptures which concern the Angel of the Lord with the first chapter of John and the verses about the Word, the Logos. We have these verses in the Gospel of John, chapter one:

"In the beginning was the Word, and the Word was with God, and the Word was God...and the Word became flesh and dwelt among us, and we saw His glory, glory as of the only begotten from the Father, full of grace and truth.

(John 1:1,14)." And then, further down the page we have these important words concerning the Word or the Logos (Greek).

"No one has seen God at any time; the only begotten God who is in the bosom of the Father, He has *explained Him*. (John 1:18)." One prominent theologian says the following:

"The Second Person, fulfilling the significant meaning of the title Logos, is, and always has been, as He ever will be, the manifestation of God. This is implied in the term Logos; for He who bears that name within the Godhead, is to the Godhead what speech is to thought—the expression of it (Lewis Sperry Chafer, Systematic Theology, volumes 3 and 4, p.12)." He says later in his writing, "As *Logos,* the Second Person has always been the self-revelation of God. ...Whenever truth about the Person of God or His message is to be disclosed—whether it be by the Angel of Jehovah or the Incarnate Son—the Second Person as *Logos* is the One who reveals (Chafer, p.21)."

NEVER IN THE NEW TESTAMENT

In connection with this is the fact that the term "The Angel of the Lord" occurs only in the Old Testament. Again, we say, that specific terminology is found only in the Old Testament, not in the New. In the New Testament we read of Gabriel speaking to Mary and later in Jude, verse 9 we read of Michael, the archangel. In Matthew 1:21 we read of **"<u>an angel of the Lord</u>"** speaking to Joseph and in Luke 2:9 we read of **"<u>an angel</u>**

of the Lord" (Emphasis mine) announcing the birth of Jesus to shepherds. But a reference to "an angel of the Lord" is not the same as "The Angel of the Lord," The latter terminology is not found in the New Testament record. There is a reason for that: The Word has become incarnate. The **"Word became flesh (John 1:14)."** The Son of God came to earth and lived as a man, though still being the Son of God. He walked among men, not as the Angel of the Lord, but as the Word Incarnate. Therefore, as long as Jesus Christ walked among us, there is no need for an appearance of The Angel of the Lord. The truth about the Word, as stated in John 1:18, along with the fact that the Angel in Rev. chapter 10 is holding the scroll, leads me to believe that the majestic person now holding that book is none other than "The Angel of the Lord" of the Old Testament.

And I saw another strong angel coming down out of heaven, clothed with a cloud; "and the rainbow was upon his head, and his face was like the sun, and his feet like pillars of fire; **and he had in his hand a little book which was open. (Rev. 10:1,2)."** Let me say just a bit more about this verse that speaks of the fact that He is "**clothed with a cloud and the rainbow was upon His head** (Rev; 10:1)."

Writer J.A. Seiss, in his commentary on Revelation entitled "The Apocalypse" writes the following:

> "The attire of this angel indicates Deity. John beholds him *'clothed about with a cloud.'* Whenever clouds are connected with glorious

manifestations, there we find the presence of Divinity. If there is a cloud, there is mystery; and if there is mystery, there is suggestion of Deity. The Lord descended on Mount Sinai in a *thick cloud*. He appeared on the mercy-seat in *a cloud*. When Israel was delivered, 'the Lord went before them by day in a *pillar of cloud*. When the glory of the Lord filled the tabernacle, 'a cloud covered the tent of the congregation.' When God reproached Israel for their murmurings, 'the glory of the Lord appeared in a cloud.' 'The Lord said to Moses. Lo, I come unto thee in a thick cloud.' The Psalmist gives it as the characteristic of the Almighty, that '*clouds* and darkness are round about Him.' ...that He maketh the *clouds* His chariot. ...When the King of Glory cometh in His divine majesty to judge the earth, the exclamation is, 'Behold He cometh with *clouds.*' Clouds therefore, belong to the attire of Deity... No mere angel is ever arrayed in such drapery, and the vision is that of the glorious God-man Himself, in the midst of the grand administration of judgment." [Seiss p. 224]

Seiss goes on to speak about "the rainbow." He points out that it does not speak of <u>a</u> rainbow but rather <u>the</u> rainbow. "We saw this rainbow back in the fourth chapter, where it is given as one of the grand appurtenances of the throne [Seiss,p. 224]."

We read in chapter 4 of Revelation, "**And He who was sitting was like a jasper stone and a sardius in appearance; and *there was* a rainbow around the throne, like an emerald in appearance (Rev. 4:3)."** With these words Seiss adds to my thinking the thought that this is no ordinary angel, who is about to bring His judgment on earth to a grand climax.

HAGAR—THE EGYPTIAN MAID

This brings us now to the very first reference to the Angel of the Lord in the Scriptural record. In Genesis chapter 16 we have the account of a major domestic problem taking place in the home of Abram and Sarai. Because they were still without the promised "son" we read that they took on themselves a means of bringing a child into their home. We read in Genesis 16:3, "**After Abram had lived ten years in the land of Canaan, Abram's wife Sarai took Hagar the Egyptian, her maid, and gave her to her husband Abram as his wife."**

We then read, "**He went in to Hagar, and she conceived; and when she saw that she had conceived, her mistress was despised in her sight (Gen. 16:4)."** Now there is major tension in the home which results in Hagar running away from the harsh treatment that was coming from Sarai.

Now we have the first reference to the Angel of the Lord in the Bible, whom we believe to be the Second Person of the trinity. The Son of God, the one who was to become our Savior finds Hagar by a spring of water in the wilderness. He tells her to return to Sarai and to the place of submission in that home. The Angel of the Lord proceeds them to comfort her with a promise saying, "**I will greatly multiply your descendants so that they will be too many to count (Gen. 16:10.**" Then we read, "**Moreover, the angel of the Lord said to her further, 'Behold you are with child, and you will bear a son; and you shall call his name Ishmael, because the Lord has given heed to your affliction (Gen. 16:11).'**" So then, we have here in the early pages of the Bible an account of the Son of God meeting with an Egyptian maid so as to bring her comfort with the promise of a child.

That which is now important to our study is her reaction to the presence of this Divine messenger: **"Then she called the name of the LORD who spoke to her, 'You are a God who sees;' for she said, 'Have I even remained alive here after seeing Him** (Gen.16:13)?'" Notice that the word **"LORD"** is in capital letters in our English translations, indicating that the Hebrew word here is **"Yahweh."** It then is obvious that the words here do not refer to a mere angel, but to God Himself. We then read that Hagar wonders why she is still alive after seeing the One she believes to be God Himself. **"Have I even remained alive here after seeing Him** (Genesis 16:13)?"

The above story presents to us the wonderful truth that the Son of God, who was to become Jesus our Savior, is seen very early in the Scriptural account, as ministering to and comforting people. He is the Logos, the Word, communicating the nature of the God we worship. As Hagar declares in Gen. 16:13, **"You are a God who sees."**

All of this is to say that I have no trouble believing that the great Angel of Rev. 10:1 is the Angel of the Lord of the Old Testament. He is the Son of God, the Lamb of God, and the Lion of the tribe of Judah.

I must add here that many modern-day Bible commentators do not go along with this thinking. People like Hal Lindsay, John Walvoord, W.A. Crisswell, Robert Thomas and a number of others believe that the great person in this account is a majesty angel, like a Michael or Gabriel, who is acting as an ambassador representing the Son of God. Just as with regard to our American ambassadors serving around the world represent, each one, the president of the United States, so Jesus Christ has here a majestic ambassador representing Himself in the act of taking possession of planet earth. Like some of the older commentators like J. A. Seiss, Walter Kelly or William Scott, I take the position as stated above that the Lamb of God <u>Himself</u> is the one serving the title-deed to the inhabitants of planet earth.

I add to my argument the wording of scripture in Matthew 17 where we have Moses and Elijah appearing with Jesus on the Mount of Transfiguration. We read, **"And He was transfigured before them and His face shone like the sun, and His garments became as white as light (Mathew 17:2)."** This is very like what we have in Rev. 10:1 **"and his face was**

like the sun, and his feet like pillars of fire." Again, we have the description of Christ as found in Rev. chapter one, some of which reads, **"...and His face was like the sun shining in its strength (Rev. 1:16),"** or **"His feet were like burnished bronze, when it has been made to glow as in a furnace (Rev. 1:15)."**

But enough said as to whether it is Christ Himself or His ambassador, we have here in Rev. chapter 10 a grand picture of the Lion of the tribe of Judah moving to take possession of what was first created and then redeemed.

CHAPTER SEVENTEEN

THE GRAND MOMENT

We come now to the climactic moment in the story that began back in chapter five when the Lamb of God received the book (scroll) from the Father's hand. We read concerning the mighty angel who, we believe, is the Lord Jesus Christ. We read:

> **"...and he had in his hand a little book which was open. He placed his right foot on the sea and his left on the land; and he cried out with a loud voice, as when a lion roars; and when he had cried out, the seven peals of thunder uttered their voices (Revelation 10:2-3)."**

Back in Rev. 5:6 it is the Lamb of God who takes the book from the hand of the One who is on the throne. Now it is the lion who roars (the Lion of the tribe of Judah?) and **"cries out with a loud voice and declares that 'there will be delay no longer (Rev. 10:6).'"** "Delay no longer" probably is a better translation than "**time no longer**" as rendered in the Old King James Version.

By way of review, we suggested that "the main story" or "the heart of the book" of Revelation begins in chapter 5 and extends through chapter 10. Beginning in chapter 11 of Revelation we have another version of the story with more of the details of this period revealed.

"**And they said to me 'You must prophesy again concerning many peoples and nations and tongues and kings (Rev. 10:11).'**" We have surveyed the contents of chapters six, seven, eight, and nine of Revelation devoting space to what we deem to be important with regard to presenting the main story without getting bogged down in all the details.

Now we come to the grand moment. It is grand and momentous beyond our ability to describe. Jesus Christ is about to take possession of that which He has created and redeemed. The usurper, the devil, is about to be completely vanquished. All of the evil and misery that has fallen upon this world must now come to an end. Our Savior is about to take hold of that which is rightfully His. Now the time has finally come. As He says "**there will be no more delay (Rev. 10:6).**"

ON THE SEA, AND ON THE LAND

Now we must go back to the Old Testament, where one can read of events and words that foreshadow that which is presented in Rev. chapter 10. Back in the book of Deuteronomy the Lord God instructs His people through Moses in this way:

> **"Every place on which the <u>sole of your foot treads</u> shall be yours; your border will be from the wilderness to Lebanon and from the river Euphrates, as far as the western sea. No man will be able to stand before you; the LORD your God will lay the dread of you on all the land on which <u>you set foot</u>, as He has spoken (Deut. 11:24-25)." [Emphasis mine]**

After the death of Moses, the promise is repeated in the first chapter of the book of Joshua. **"Moses my servant is dead; now therefore arise, cross this Jordan, you and all this people, to the land which I am giving to them, to the sons of Israel. <u>Every place on which the sole of your foot treads, I have given it to you, just as I spoke to Moses (Joshua 1:2-3)." [Emphasis mine]**

In chapter six of Joshua, we read of the battle of Jericho. You may recall that the people of Israel are instructed to march around the city of Jericho for six days and then on the seventh day they are to march around the city seven times and the priests are to blow the trumpets (Joshua 6:3.4). **"It shall be that when they make a long blast with the ram's horn, and when you hear the sound of the trumpet, all the people will shout; and the wall of the city will fall down flat, and the people will go up every man straight ahead (Joshua 6:5)."**

I believe we need to connect the promise of chapter one of Joshua with the battle of Jericho. **"Every place the sole of your foot shall tread I have given it to you (Josh. 1:3)."** At Jericho they are to <u>tread</u> on the ground surrounding the city. That is, they march on that ground. In doing so they are saying in so many words, "According to the promises of the LORD, this city belongs to us. This land will fall to Joshua." [paraphrase mine] I believe that this is the meaning of the instruction that is given to them, in that they are to march around the city so many times. They are laying claim to that ancient real estate.

I believe that the Battle of Jericho, as well as being history, is looking ahead to the time when Christ will lay claim to this world. We remember that, interesting enough, Joshua is the Old Testament name for Jesus, one name is Hebrew, the other is Greek. They both mean, "Yahweh is salvation." We now read that this majestic person places His right foot on the sea and His left foot on the land. He is placing the soles of His feet on planet earth, taking possession of that which rightfully belongs to Him. The Lion of the tribe of Judah cries out with a loud voice as did the people shout at Jericho, and the thunders roll. We can almost hear the walls of Jericho crashing down.

Three times we read in this passage that the Angel is standing on the sea and on the earth. We have it in verse 2, verse 5 and verse 8 of Rev. chapter 10. This is by way of emphasis, I believe. The seven thunders roll but John is told to seal up what the thunders have spoken. He is not to write what happens on earth when the seven thunders **utter their voices** (Rev. 10:4).

Verse 7 of Rev. chapter 10 is significant, **"but in the days of the voice of the seventh angel when he is as about to sound, then the mystery of God is finished, as He preached to His servants the prophets."** This leads me to believe that we are near the end of our story. We are at the place of God's final judgments on this world. Devout children of God have been praying and asking for many years, "How long will this world be under the control of the evil one, how long will evil prevail?" Here we read that one day that mystery will be finished.

CHAPTER EIGHTEEN

CONCLUSION

THE FATHER'S GIFT TO THE SON

"**The Revelation of Jesus Christ, which <u>God gave Him</u> to show the things which must soon take place, and He sent and communicated it by His angel to His bond-servant John. (Rev. 1:1).**" [Emphasis mine] The Greek word for "Revelation" is "apokalupsis" from which we get the English word "apocalypse." The verb means to pull away the veil, it's an uncovering. [W.E. Vine, "Vine's Expository Dictionary of Old and New Testament words," p. 964.] More importantly, it is seen here as the Father's gift to the Son. And yet, many pastors in our churches hesitate to approach the book.

Furthermore, there is the promised blessing stated in verse 3 of Rev. chapter 1: "**Blessed is he who reads and those who hear the words of the prophecy, and heed the things which are written in it; for the time is near.**" The "blessing" is promised and yet there are many in our churches who never get near the book. It is deemed by many as incomprehensible or just plain weird.

In this writing I have tried to share a part of the book that is comprehensible and worthy of thought. I began with the story of a man who bought a farm and with title-deed in hand had to engage in a fierce battle so as to drive out the former tenant and take possession of that which he had paid for and was rightfully his. I have tried to show that chapters 5-10 tell a similar story and comprise the heart, or the main part of the book. I have tried to make it understandable for the average believer. It is a story that has brought a blessing to my own heart. My Savior is going to take possession of that which He has redeemed by His own precious blood. That brings a blessing to my own heart, even though much of the material has to do with the sinfulness of this world and the judgment that is due them. The story begins when the Lamb of God is deemed worthy to take the book from the Father's hand and begins to open the seals. It ends when the seventh trumpet sounds and seven thunders utter their voices and God's final judgments fall on a sinful rebellious world. While it is true that I have not tried to get into the meaning of every verse, I trust that I have conveyed the main story of the book of Revelation in a way that can be understood.

In the first section of this writing, I have shared a number of the stories that are found on God's appointment calendar, some from the book of Acts and some from my own life. One of the common denominators of these stories is that people were moving toward God before the appointment takes place. Our Sovereign God was drawing people to Himself and then setting up an appointment for a servant of His to meet with them. Philip was sent to the Ethiopian. Peter was sent to Cornelius and Paul was sent to meet with Lydia on the bank of a river in Philippi. I have suggested that we should be open to what He may be doing in our lives. Perhaps He is sending someone our way for us to influence for Him in some way. The nature of God's calendar is such that we cannot see the appointments before-hand. We recognize them after the fact and then praise Him for what He has done.

In the second section of this writing, we have looked into the appointment that Jesus has with this world in the end times. He has an appointment with this world so as to bring judgment upon it. He has told us that we cannot know the hour of His Second Coming. Someday in glory, we will be able to look back upon it, comprehend it more fully so as to worship and praise Him more than we thought possible.

I have shared with the reader the story of the 144,000 sons of Israel that will come to Christ during those dark days. They all will have had some kind of special appointment with Him, so as a whole, they become the "first-fruits to God" during those times. They have a song to sing that no one else can learn. We are not privileged to know exactly how they come to Christ, but in an experience that each of them will have, His name and that of His Father will be written on their forehead. (See our treatment of chapters seven and fourteen of the Book of Revelation concerning them.) God has in these chapters told us about these future appointments, but we cannot look into His appointment calendar to know exactly when these things will be.

It's been a personal blessing for me to think about Jesus having His ultimate victory over sin and the evils of this world. It's also been a special blessing for me to think about God's future meetings with the 144,000 and a multitude of others who will come to Him. Just how God brought them to Himself, we are not told. Had they begun to seek Him? Or did some them have a special meeting with Christ Himself, as did Paul on the road to Damascus? Perhaps, some day we will know.

APPENDIX SECTION

Dear reader, you have finished reading this book- that is, the main part of the book. For those who would like to read or study further on some of the matters brought up in the writing, you may now consider some or all of the essays found in this Appendix Section.

A BRIEF ESSAY ON ELECTION AND FREE WILL

Pursuant to a major argument of this writing.

It was my senior year at a Christian Liberal Arts college. I had decided to major in philosophy, partly because I was influenced by the professor who was the chairman of the philosophy department. He was brilliant. In his presentation of deep subjects and Christian values he excelled. I liked him a lot. I wanted to study under him. So, under him and the other professors in the department I studied men like Socrates, Plato and Aristotle, as well as more recent writers. I read the works of Immanuel Kant and others and concluded that it all really didn't matter much. There didn't seem to be certain answers as to the meaning of life. But it was good for me to learn a discipline of reading and thinking. There were also valuable courses on Christian Apologetics, Ethics (We did a whole semester on a study of the Ten Commandments) and Values.

Looking back on it many years later, I believe that the Lord guided me into the right decision.

A WEEK- LONG DISCUSSION ON ELECTION AND FREE WILL.

I believe it was towards the end of my senior year when the professor, the man I mentioned before, led us in a week-long discussion of election/predestination as opposed to free will. It was an extensive exercise of thinking and exchanging thoughts between the teacher and the students. But I remember what the professor said at the very end of the week. He said something like this, "Both seem to be true. The Bible seems to teach that both Election and Free Will are true. But whatever you do, don't rob God of His glory." This is, even now, of interest to me in view of the fact that he had said in so many words that he was a modified Calvinist.

After so many years of thinking and studying the Word of God as a Bible-teaching pastor, I now believe that he was right; both are true. You may say, "How can that be? If we are the elect, the chosen of God, how is that we may choose to receive Jesus as our Savior and Lord? "It doesn't seem to be logical," you say.

And I say, "I don't understand the Trinity either." It doesn't seem logical that one can be three and three can be one. Yet the Bible clearly teaches it.

I still believe both are true, and it's not because I am still under the influence of the man I admired. Let me share some thoughts on the matter that I entertain: We read in John 6:44, **"No one can come to Me, unless the Father who sent Me draws him..."** Can I easily accept that? Yes. Of course. We notice also the words of John 17:6 as Jesus is in prayer to His Father, **"I have manifested your name to the men whom you gave out of the world; they were Yours and You gave them to Me, and they have kept your word."** The emphasis of this verse is that those who come to believe in Christ are a gift from the Father to the Son. Three times in that verse the word "gave" is used. It is easy to match this with John 6:44, **"No one can come to Me, unless the Father who sent Me draws him..."** The Father, through the work of the Spirit is preparing the gift for His Son.

But now, what about John 7:17? **"If anyone is willing to do His will, he will know of the teaching, whether it is of God, or whether I speak from Myself."** The beginning of the verse can be read. **"If anyone chooses to do His will ... (John 7:17."** Can I readily accept the wording of that verse? Of Course. What I cannot go along with is the person who reads this and says, "Yeah, But! It is God who is pulling the strings." And if I come to the place where I am in love with Jesus Christ, is that love of myself, or is God pulling the strings? What kind of love is it that-- if it is not freely given? Does God even want us to love Him because He controls us? These are not easy questions to answer. Is our God programing us to respond to Him in genuine love?

THE INTEGRITY OF SCRIPTURE VERSES

I believe we must honor the meaning of the words, God's words. If you say, "Yeah, But!" you are contradicting what the words say. You can't say "yes, but no." You just can't wipe out the meaning of the verse.

We mention again Jeremiah 29:13. **"You will seek Me and find Me, when you search for Me with all your heart."** But someone says, "Yeah, but." It seems to say that one can seek Him, but that's impossible because we are **"dead in our trespasses and sins"** (Ephesians 2:1). It seems to me that we do better to take these promises at their face value. Why am I stressing this? In this writing we have been considering Bible stories of people who were seeking God. But there are some who say that my observations are not valid because of the doctrine of predestination

THE SOVEREIGNTY OF GOD IN THE EPISTLES

Let's now look at the other side of the matter. It has always been of some interest to me that Peter and Paul put the matter of God's sovereignty right out front. Notice what Paul has to say at the beginning of his epistle to the Ephesians.

> **"Blessed be the God and Father of our Lord Jesus Christ, who has blessed us with every spiritual blessing in the heavenly places in Christ, just as He chose us before the**

foundation of the world, that we would be holy and blameless before Him. In love He predestined us to adoption through Jesus Christ to Himself, according to the kind intention of His will, to the praise of the glory of His grace which He freely bestowed on us in the Beloved (Ephesians 1:3-6)."

According to Paul, God chose us before the foundation of the world. Now notice what Peter does in the first chapter of his first epistle.

"Peter, an apostle of Jesus Christ to those who reside as aliens, scattered throughout Pontus, Galatia, Cappadocia, Asia, and Bithynia, who are chosen according to the foreknowledge of God the Father, by the sanctifying work of the Spirit, to obey Jesus Christ and be sprinkled with His blood: May grace and peace be yours in the fullest measure (I Peter 1:1-2)."

Many volumes have been dedicated to solving the problem of election and free will. This has been a very brief essay so as to defend the main argument of my writing. Here is an interesting quotation from The Moody Handbook of Theology concerning the Calvinistic doctrine of predestination and election we read, "The reason many reject these doctrines is that they suppose the doctrines exclude human responsibility. However, most Calvinists recognize the antimony (the seeming contradiction of biblical teaching about both God's sovereignty and human responsibility), and they live with it as a <u>divine paradox</u>. [p. 485] (Emphasis mine)." So that is where we started when we began this essay; the Bible seems to teach both election and free will.

SOMETHING VERY PROFOUND FROM PAUL

Let me close by referring to something very remarkable in the words of Paul that are found in II Timothy. Paul exhorts in verse 1 of chapter 2 of II Timothy: **"You therefore my son, be strong in the grace that is in Christ Jesus."** He says also in verses 3 and 4 of II Tim. chapter 2, **"Suffer hardship with me, as a good soldier of Christ Jesus. No soldier in active service entangles himself in the affairs of everyday life, so that he may please the one who enlisted him as a soldier."**

He goes on to mention the athlete and the hard-working farmer, speaking as to the value of hardship and training. Now we come to the remarkable statement made by Paul concerning himself, **"Remember Jesus Christ, risen from the dead, descended of David, according to my gospel, for which I suffer hardship even to imprisonment as a criminal; but the word of God is not imprisoned. For this reason, I endure all things for the sake of those who are chosen, so that they may obtain the salvation which is in Christ Jesus and with it, eternal glory (II Timothy 2:8-10)."** Paul has within him a deep passion for those who are chosen- that is the elect, that they might obtain salvation [emphasis mine]. Paul does not place the matter of election on the back burner. It and the sovereignty of God are very much a part of his being. Likewise, we are not ashamed of the doctrine.

ACCORDING TO THE KNOWLEDGE OF GOD

In the epistle of I Peter chapter one we have the following words, **"Peter an apostle of Jesus Christ, to those who reside as aliens, scattered throughout Pontus ...who are chosen according to the foreknowledge of God the Father, by the sanctifying work of the Spirit, to obey Jesus Christ ... (I Peter 1:1-3)."** Emphasis mine]

Let us now consider an attempt to harmonize the tensions between the matters of "election" and "freewill" by someone esteemed in the studies of theology, John F. Walvoord. Dr. Walvoord was president of Dallas Theological Seminary and chairman of the Department of Theology when he gave a classroom lecture to us, ca. 1962. He presented to us an interesting approach seeking to reconcile those two words found in I Peter 1:2 and 3: chosen and foreknowledge. On the chalk board at the front of the class he drew a long series of parallel lines. He labeled them A B C E F and so on throughout the length of the diagram.

He said that each line represented a possible alternative plan existing from before the foundation of the world. These possible plans would all be presented before the mind of God with respect to His infinite wisdom and knowledge. Please note our diagram below: Does He proceed with plan A or B or E, etc., or go with a plan not represented on our diagram that is far beyond our limited imagination?

A --

B--

C--

D.--

E--

F--

G--

We have drawn only a few lines, but in God's mind we can imagine an infinite number of lines representing plans for the universe. The emphasis now is on foreknowledge. God knows what the future would hold for each and every course of action on His part.

So, let's use our imagination. In plan D God could have created Mars as the perfect place for humans to live. Perhaps there would have been no need for a Garden of Eden. Sin never enters the situation. Now with regard to each option God knows perfectly what the outcome will be down through the years as well as at the end of years.

Let's now talk about planet earth. In plan C there would be no need for a Garden of Eden because man and woman would have been fine without it. Or, there would be no need for it because there would be no sin. Sin is not allowed. Man is not made in the image of God and does not have free will. Man does not come to love God out of free will. What kind of love would it be if man has no choice? Does God want to be loved that way? In that case man is not much more than a robot. Some ask, "Why did God allow sin to enter the world?" The answer has to do with man having free will. [Dear reader please note that I am paraphrasing what Dr. Walvoord said in his lecture. That was many years ago and I cannot remember exactly what he said, only the essence of it.]

In plan D there is a Garden of Eden but the people are different, not Adam and Eve, but another couple. And there is no Cain and no Abel. Other people are involved and the serpent is not allowed anywhere near the garden.

In plan F the descendants of the first couple are very different than what we have today. Sin has entered the world and Spirit of God is not restraining lawlessness. The result is absolute chaos and the destruction of that world.

Now let's assume that we are in plan G. Man has been made in the image of God and is capable of fellowship with God in the areas of intellect, emotion and will. But sin has entered the world and man has lost his ability to love God and follow after God until he is born again by the Spirit of God. Now, our point is, that God perfectly knew all of this would happen. Looking on down through the years He knows that this man will seek God and this man will not. This woman will serve God but this other will not. Some ask, "How can anyone choose for God if he or she is dead in trespasses and sins?" Good question. Some say there is what is called "Prevenient Grace." That is to say that even though they are dead spiritually, God in His grace awakens them enough so that they can choose Him or reject Him. In plan G a man named Joe trusts in Christ as his Savior, but that is according to the foreknowledge of God. However, it was predetermined long ago when God proceeded to go with plan G.

Yes, I have added some of of my own words to those of Dr. Walvoord. But his point in that lecture was: God goes ahead with a plan that includes freewill for man. But the fact that He went ahead with that plan predestines the outcome. Therefore, the Sovereignty of God and the freewill of man are both included. Both God's foreknowledge and man's free will are included. Now I know that the approached stated above will not satisfy everyone. In fact, I have shared this with people who find ways to object. But it gives us something to think about when we recognize that, as said before, the Bible seems to teach both "election" and "free will." The above represents a possible solution as to how both can be true.

Let's conclude our consideration by noting part of that which Peter preached on the Day of Pentecost. Referring to Jesus Peter said, **"...this man, delivered over** by **the predetermined plan and foreknowledge of God, you nailed to a cross by the hands of godless men and put Him to death** (Acts 2:23)." That is what we all need to acknowledge and cherish in our hearts and minds. I remember what my professor said at the end of our discussion, "Whatever you do, don't rob God of His glory."

APPENDIX II

FINDING GOD'S WILL

Pursuant to our consideration of the struggles of the apostle Paul finding God's direction on his second missionary journey.

PROVERBS 3:5-6

"Trust in the Lord with all your heart and do not lean on your own understanding. In all your ways acknowledge Him and He will make your paths straight (Proverbs 3:5-6)."

Imagine that you are traveling down a highway, either in a car or on foot- it doesn't matter, and you know that you will be coming to a fork in the road. You will need to make a decision as to the way you will go, to the left or to the right. The fork in the road may be a great distance down the road, or it may be close. How will I know which one is the path of God's will for me? I literally had such an experience and it was for me an interesting one. I was on an inter-state highway and I was coming to a choice as to which way to go. Should I continue straight on that road or should I take the next exit off that road? Which one would be right for me, the one which would be in accordance with the will of God? -more about that later.

In our chapter on Lydia, the business woman in Philippi, we considered the matter of Paul and his travels. Paul would eventually arrive in Philippi, and then Thessalonica, and Berea, and Athens, and finally Corinth on this, his second missionary journey, but it would be with difficulty and a struggle that Paul found God's way in the matter. We noted in our discussion there that Paul intended first to visit the places where he had been on his first missionary journey and then proceed North and East into Proconsular Asia. But God wanted him to head west. It was quite a struggle. Paul became very ill and he refers to it in his letter to the Galatians, chapter 4:12-14. Because of that illness Paul was unable to go where he wanted to go. We read in Acts 16:6 that in Asia **"they were forbidden by the Spirit to speak the word."**

After that we read in Acts 16:7 that Spirit of Jesus did not permit them **"they were trying to go into Bithynia, and the "Spirit of Jesus did not permit them**." As we mentioned in the writing of that chapter, we read these words but we do not know exactly how the Spirit of God was directing Paul.

Finally, as recorded in verses 9 and 10 of Acts 16 we read of the vision in the night that directly guided him on the way he should go, **"A vision appeared to Paul in the night, a man of**

Macedonia was standing and appealing to him, and saying, 'Come over to Macedonia and help us.' When we had seen the vision, immediately we sought to go into Macedonia, concluding that God had called us to preach the gospel to them."

In Acts 16 we have this interesting account of how Paul struggled to find the way that God wanted him to go. We note that the Holy Spirit was very much involved. But then there was that decisive vision in the night. The question is, how do we find God's will for us today? On some rare occasion there might be granted to some man or woman a vision that shows them the way to go. I would not exclude that possibility. Most definitely we must not, as Paul says in I Thessalonians 5:19 "**quench the Spirit**," that is by saying, "no" to his influence in our lives. Furthermore, we must not grieve the Holy Spirit as is mentioned in Ephesians 4:30, "**Do not grieve the Holy Spirit of God, by whom you were sealed for the day of redemption**." How do we grieve the Holy Spirit? We do that by allowing unconfessed sin to continue in our lives. The context of Eph. 4:30 makes that very clear. Beginning in verse 25 of Ephesians chapter 4 we have a long list of sins which grieve the person of the Holy Spirit within us and which, by the way, hinder us from finding God's will:

> "**Therefore, laying aside falsehood, SPEAK TRUTH EACH ONE OF YOU WITH HIS NEIGHBOR, for we are members of one**

another. BE ANGRY AND yet DO NOT SIN; do not let the sun go down on your anger, and do not give the devil an opportunity. He who steals must steal no longer; but rather he must labor, performing with his own hands what is good, so that he will have something to share with one who has need. Let no unwholesome word proceed from your mouth, but only such a word as is good for edification according to the need of the moment, so that it will give grace to those who hear (Ephesians 4:25-29)."

That is the immediate context of Paul's admonition to **"grieve not the Holy Spirit of God (Ephesians 4:30)."** It would seem to be obvious that sin in the life would hinder the guidance of the Holy Spirit in our lives. I have read books and articles on decision making and God's will that suggests that finding God's will is really a matter of finding guidance from what is said in Scripture. What does the Bible say? Some seem to suggest that it doesn't matter what Bible college you attend, or what job you take, or even whom you choose as a marriage partner, as long as you don't go against what is revealed in Scripture (to give some examples). But my question to them is, "Is that all there is to walking close to God? Are you saying that God does not have an opinion on colleges or jobs or someone I might want to marry?" Of course, He does have opinions and those would be based on His omniscience. I believe He knows what is best for me and that He wants what is best for me. I want to walk with Him, and to be guided by Him as to what is best for me. I have in mind one book I read on finding God's will for your life that doesn't even mention the matter of "faith." Whereas the beginning of the Proverbs 3:5-6 passage reads **"Trust in the Lord with all your heart... (Proverbs 3:5)"**

THREE KEY FACTORS

I suggest now three important steps in decision making so as to determine God's will in a matter:

First -Deliberate Prayer - This doesn't necessarily mean a long prayer, although it might mean spending a good deal of time in His presence. Rather, one needs to be deliberate in prayer, pointedly and specifically placing the matter before God. It could be a short prayer or a long prayer depending on the situation.

Secondly -Sincere Submission – Sincerity is the key word here. As you pray to the Lord about a decision you must make, you tell Him that you are completely willing to go either way in the situation. Noting the example of a fork in the road, you say to Him, "Lord, I am willing to go to the left or go to the right. In spite of my preferences, or what I might want to do, Lord, I believe you know what is best. In my heart I am willing to go whatever way You want me to go." That is the kind of sincerity in your heart that you must have. It seems that some people have more difficulty in this than others. Some seem to be controlled more by their emotions. They know what they want to do in the matter and they are inclined to do it. Perhaps some should begin by praying, "Lord, help me be sincere in this matter. Help me submit to your will."

Thirdly -Faith -This is faith that the Lord will work this out and you will end up on the right road. You may consult with friends. You may read up on the matter. You might take a piece of paper and make a list of pros and cons. Here is a list of reasons why it would be good to go this way, and here is a list of reasons why I should not. Also, there might be the factor of open or closed doors. Perhaps an open or closed door might present itself to you and influence your decision. But during the process you are believing that God is in control of the result because you have sincerely prayed to Him about it. And the amazing thing is, later on you realize that you have found the right road.

A SIMPLE ILLUSTRATION

Allow me dear reader to share some of my own experiences in this matter. One Saturday morning, on a beautiful June day, after having made a hospital visit in a nearby town, I was driving north on an interstate highway intending to head home. Normally I would proceed to a certain exit, leave the interstate and head east, back toward home and the church where I was the pastor. It was a Saturday and therefore the day when customarily I would finalize my sermon preparation for Sunday. It was an important day of thinking and praying so as to be ready to share the Word of God with my congregation on Sunday. Some pastors take Saturdays off, having done all the sermon preparation before-hand. But for me, Saturday was an all-important day in my sermon preparation.

But on this Saturday morning there came to my mind the fact that the church's soft ball team was involved in a tournament further north and to the west. I thought to myself, "it's a beautiful day, I would enjoy spending a little time there watching the guys compete with the other teams that would be there. What should I do?" This is what I did. I followed the steps that I outlined above as to following God's will.

So, I deliberately prayed about it, telling the Lord that I was willing to go either way. I would turn right off the interstate and proceed east to my study at the church, if that is what He wanted me to do. I prayed while driving, with my eyes open of course. I told the Lord as sincerely as I could that I would go whichever way He wanted me to go.

I have shared this story with young couples in marriage counseling, discussing decision making and the will of God in the marriage relationship. After telling them of my prayer time while driving that day, I ask them this question, "Which way do you think I went on that day? Did I turn east off the interstate and head back to church or did I go straight and turn left at a later exit?" Almost always they would say that I went back to the church and prepared for Sunday morning. They considered me to be a responsible person who would resist the temptation of a ball game. But the truth is, I went to the ball game and that is what makes this a good illustration. I was sincere with the Lord and therefore by faith enjoyed peace of mind at the games. I went home later that day and had no problem at all completing my sermon preparation for the next day. I felt good as I drove to the soft-ball tournament that day, because I had faith in the process. Because I had been sincere in my prayer as I drove up the highway, I knew I was on the right road.

A MORE SERIOUS MATTER

Late one evening I was at the same hospital that I mentioned before. I was on their second floor visiting a man who was seriously ill. His heart was very weak. His wife was there tending to him as best she could. However, there were many other people there as well, too many people. It seemed at the time that there were just too many people in the room. I wanted to have a quiet intimate conversation with this man concerning spiritual things. Of course, most of the people in the room were just hospital staff people doing their jobs. They kept coming in and going out. It was not a quiet, peaceful situation where I could have a serious conversation with this man about Christ.

I wanted him to know that by trusting in Jesus as his savior he could have that special peace of mind knowing that he was going to Heaven. But it was just too busy and noisy for such a conversation to take place.

Finally, I gave up on the matter. I had a word of prayer with him; it was a good-prayer, I think, but not the kind I really wanted to share with the man, and said good-bye to this man and his wife and left the room. I went downstairs to an empty lobby. Since it was now quite late in the evening; not a soul was there in that large darkened room. I decided to sit down and pray. I sat quietly there by myself and prayed, "Lord, what do you want me to do? It's late and perhaps I should just go home. Oh Lord, do you want me to go back up to that room?" After a little bit of time, I went to elevator and went back up to the man's room. I am sure they were surprised to see me reenter the room. To my pleasant surprise, the room was now empty of all the employees that had been there before. It was just the man and his wife. So, now I was able to carefully explain God's plan of salvation. After a while I again led in prayer, but now it was to the point and I was hopeful that this man was understanding what I was saying. He did not come to faith in those moments, but I felt good about my visit with him.

I went home that evening feeling led by the Lord concerning my decision to go back up to that room. In the morning I received a call from the wife. She told me that soon after I left, her husband passed way. She also told me that after I left and when they were alone, the man did pray to receive Christ as his Savior. I will always cherish the memory of that evening many years ago, when I sat in an empty lobby and asked the Lord whether I should go back up to that man's room or not. I know that the Lord can direct our paths when we pray that we might know His will. After all, logically speaking, how can He not be willing to reveal to us His will? I could tell a number of stories, some personal in nature concerning health, finances, insurance, etc., that are probably not appropriate to share at this time; but I can testify that when I have been faithful to sincerely seek His direction in a matter, He has not failed me. My faith has been greatly strengthened in this regard. Concerning the man at the hospital I have since then wondered, "What if I had not been submissive to God's will and not gone back to speak with him? What then?"

"IN ALL YOUR WAYS ACKNOWLEDGE HIM (Proverbs 3:6)."

Concerning the phrase, "In all your ways (Proverbs 3:6a…)." I take this to mean that every aspect of your life, big decisions and small decisions are to be included. It may apply as to whether or not to buy a certain item from the shelf at Walmart or, of course, the "big decisions." When we acknowledge His presence and His will in the everyday details of life, we are walking with the Lord. The tendency for most of us is to forget to take things to Him in prayer. With us it's almost automatic, to assume, "I can handle this matter by myself." That is when we are prone to make mistakes to one degree or another.

A BIG DECISION, AFTER ALL

It happened some time ago in a Howard Johnson's restaurant. (Remember those?) My wife and I were dining with a couple that we had known for some time. In fact, I had officiated at their wedding ceremony. When my wife left the table to go to the powder room, they said they wanted to share something with me. The wife said, "Pastor, we have something to tell you. My husband has had a vasectomy. We decided that two kids were enough and a family of four was just fine." I cannot remember the exact words that they used to explain their reasoning to me.

My reaction was, "Did you pray about it?" I didn't verbalize the question, but that was my thinking at the time. I did not want to embarrass them or to be confrontational. But I thought, perhaps God had a grand purpose for that next child, the one they now could not have. To be fair, perhaps they did sincerely pray about it. Perhaps it was according to His will. I am using this as an example of how many people make such decisions in life. Sometimes it never occurs to believers in Christ to pray about such matters. I include myself in this description as to how ordinary people very often make decisions in life, some large, some small.

I have made a similar application to couples who are preparing for marriage. They sometimes ask, "Pastor, what do you believe about birth control? Should we perhaps practice it for a while so as to get grounded in our marriage and then try to have a child later on?" I call their attention to verse 6 of Proverbs chapter 3, which says "...**in all your ways acknowledge Him and He will make your paths straight**." Regarding birth control, the first thing to do is to pray about it, deliberately and sincerely. Don't leave the Lord out of your decision. Don't forget Him. I am confident that if you are truly sincere in your prayer He will "make your path smooth." (Proverbs 3:6)

I believe that the Lord wants us to talk to Him about our decisions in life. Be sincere and **"trust in the Lord will all your heart and lean not unto your own understanding... (Proverbs 3:5)."**

Recently, after writing the above words on finding God's will, I realized that there is another way of translating verse 6 of Proverbs chapter 3. Instead of reading, "In all your ways acknowledge him," it might very well be rendered, **"in all your ways submit to Him."** I was in a church looking at the Bible that was in the pew. In a particular edition of the version there was that rendering of the text. It said, **"In all your ways submit to Him... (Provers 3:5)."** I later was discussing this with a pastor friend of mine and he then did some research on it in the Hebrew language. "Yes," he said to me in so many words, "The text in the Hebrew looks like it could be taken that way."

Actually, that makes a good deal of sense. Because the problem that many people have is that of submission. We find it difficult to be honest with the Lord when we say to Him that we are willing to go either way in a matter. Sometimes, we can't suppress our feelings and desires -- that is, "what we want to do." Therefore, we need to recognize that fact in heart and mind and say, "Lord, please help me to be submissive to you in this matter. Help me to really want to do your will."

APPENDIX III

FIVE HUSBANDS

*Pursuant to our study of John chapter
four "The Meeting at the Well."*

Up until now it had been a sad story, a woman put aside,
divorced by one man after another. I believe, as said before,
in our chapter entitled, "The Meeting at Jacob's well," the
Samaritan women there was a victim of the culture of the day
and a victim of men who were prone to put away their wives for
the slightest of reasons. I am not saying that I condone all her
part in those relationships or her agreeing to live with a man
outside of marriage. But let us now consider this matter of her
having five husbands.

WHAT'S THE DIFFERENCE?

Jesus says to the woman at the well in Samaria, **"...you
have had five husbands, and the one whom you now have,
is not your husband (John 4:18)."** I have through the years,

when speaking with couples who were preparing for marriage, asked them this question: What do you think is the difference in relationship between man and woman concerning the first five men and the last? I have heard answers like this, referring to the man she is now living with, "Well, he was not a Christian." I then have pointed out that the people here are not even Jews, let alone Christians. They are Samaritans. Marriage is for all the peoples of this world. "Well, perhaps they don't really love one another." I then point out that we don't know whether or not they really love one another. Perhaps, they did. Eventually we get to the real answer. They have not entered into any kind of a real commitment. There have been no vows. There has been no ceremony involving a public recognition of a marriage relationship, whatever that was in that Samaritan culture. But then we ask, what about the first five? Was she really married five times?

THE HOLY SPIRIT DOES NOT MAKE MISTAKES

Many years ago, while in college I learned this definition of the inspiration of the Scriptures. As I recall the definition that a professor gave us goes like this: "Inspiration is that act whereby God, the Holy Spirit, gave us the Scriptures, communicating His truth to us through the agency of fallible men, yet in such a way that the product was free from error of any kind." [Exact source unknown.] I do not believe that the Holy Spirit was careless with words or made mistakes in the process of inspiring men in the process of giving us the Scriptures. I believe in verbal inspiration. That is, it extends to the very words used. If we read that Jesus refers to the first five men as "husbands," I believe that they were indeed husbands and that Jesus recognizes five marriages.

There is one technical point that we should make here. The Greek word "andros" can mean either "man" or "husband." But the former does not make sense in this verse of Scripture, John 4:18. It does not seem logical to say, "You have had five men and the one you have now is not your man." Rather, our Bible versions have it right. **"You have had five husbands, and the one whom you now have is not your husband (John 4:18)."** Jesus makes a distinction between the first five who are husbands and the last one who is not a husband. Again, my point is that Jesus recognizes five marriages. Yes, sin takes place when one marriage ends and another one begins. Perhaps there is one guilty party, perhaps there are two. But God recognizes a new union, when a new commitment has been entered into, even though sin has taken place previously. I know that some will say "no, this woman has had one husband and the last five are not husbands." So, they say, she has been living in adultery ever since she married the second man. But I don't think that is the case. What would God have her do if children have been born along the way, does she disrupt their lives and the family at the time and try to reunite with the first man? What would that do to the children? That would mean more heart-ache, more disruption of peace for all. I don't believe my God would endorse that kind of hurt on families. And I don't believe we can just ignore the words of Jesus when he states that she has had five husbands as opposed to the last relationship.

WHAT'S HER FUTURE?

Looking back to the story of the woman whom Jesus met at the well, as recorded in John chapter 4, what advice would Jesus now give her? If given the opportunity to speak with this woman, now that she has become a child of God, what does Jesus now tell her to do? Does he say that she should go back to that first man in her life, try to reunite with Him, and if that is not possible, then live as a single woman? It seems more reasonable to me that He would tell her to get married to the man she is now living with. If the man is willing, and we might assume that he has become a believer as well, then she should enter into that state of commitment that defines the marriage relationship. Yes, I know that God hates adultery because it is a violation of that which is sacred, but I also believe that we worship a God of "new beginnings." There are many Christians couples in our land today who need the assurance that God forgives sin and is a God of "new beginnings."

WHAT IS MARRIAGE?

Let us now try to define or describe what marriage is in the eyes of God. I try to consider this question also during the course of pre-marriage counselling. The classic passage on this subject is first found in Gen. 2:24, **"For this reason a man shall leave his father and his mother and be joined to his wife; and they shall become one flesh."** This verse is quoted a number of times in the New Testament. The old King James version renders part of this as "**leaving…and cleaving.**" I think that the concept of leaving both farther and mother and entering into a new relationship implies a degree of commitment to the new relationship and then we read that the man is to be joined to his wife. A man is moving from one state of relationship to another. He is leaving the family, the relationship into which he was born and nurtured by father and mother. To leave the reality of that state and enter a state of being joined to another implies commitment. The "**leaving**" and "**cleaving**" implies commitment to a new state of being. The "cleaving" implies a new and permanent state of being.

MATTHEW 19:5-6

In this passage Jesus is answering the Pharisees concerning marriage and divorce. They seem to be interested in a very liberal view of the matter, permission to divorce one's wife **for any reason at all** (Matt. 19:3)." Jesus says in verses 5-6 of Matt. 19, "' **FOR THIS REASON A MAN SHALL LEAVE HIS FATHER AND MOTHER AND BE JOINED TO HIS WIFE AND THE TWO SHALL BECOME ONE FLESH.'**

'So, they are no longer two, but one flesh. What therefore God has joined together, let no man put separate.'"

EPHESIANS 5:28,29,31

"So, husbands ought to love their own wives as their own bodies. He who loves his own wife, loves himself; no one ever hated his own flesh, but cherishes it, just as Christ also does the church, because we are members of His body. 'FOR THIS REASON, A MAN SHALL LEAVE HIS FATHER AND MOTHER AND BE JOINED TO HIS WIFE, AND THE TWO SHALL BECOME ONE FLESH. (Eph. 3:28-31).'" In this passage Paul is admonishing husbands and wives with respect to their sacred duty in the marriage relationship. The sacred nature of marriage is set forth by comparing it to the oneness of Christ and His church.

I CORINTHIANS 6:15-20

Now the apostle Paul surprises us by using Genesis 2:24 for a very different purpose. He admonishes the Christian man of the church at Corinth not to defile himself by joining himself to a prostitute. He says, **"Do you not know that the one who joins himself to a prostitute is one body *with her*? For he says, 'THE TWO SHALL BECOME ONE FLESH,' But the one who joins himself to the Lord is one spirit *with Him* (I Cor. 6:16,17)."**

But Paul is not talking about marriage, is he? The man who spends time with a prostitute may not even know her name. Yet Paul uses a portion of Genesis 2:24 and applies it here. What are we to take from this? Does such a man get married to such a woman. No, but we do learn here something about marriage. Paul is referring to that which is physical. He speaks of becoming "**one body**" with her (I Cor. 6:16). But the other part which makes up marriage is missing.

MARRIAGE HAS TWO PARTS

It seems to me that marriage has two parts, the physical and the psychological. In I Corinthians Paul refers to the "one body" of physical union between a man and a woman. For some time, I pondered as to the right word to describe the part that involves the commitment entered into by the marriage vows. Eventually I decided on the term "psychological." When a man or woman commit to the other through those marriage vows, they enter into a state of mind whereby they know that they promised themselves to one another and now belong to each other. They know that they have made promises to each other which, ideally, they intend to keep. By the term "psychological" I refer to that state of mind whereby they know that they are committed and therefore belong to each other.

A CORD WITH TWO STRANDS

Now imagine that I hold before you a cord with two strands. Now imagine that I take the two separate strands and twist them together and in doing so I make something that is very strong. Those two cords should be entwined together during that marriage relationship. The physical act of making love enhances the oneness that they have now entered into. The physical act without the psychological awareness of belonging to each other is not the same. Making love outside of marriage comes up empty by comparison.

THE MOST BEAUTIFUL PART

In speaking with a couple who are planning to get married, I often ask them this question: What will be the most beautiful part of your wedding day? Will it be the beauty of the flowers or the gowns or the special music? I then suggest to them that the most beautiful part of the ceremony is seen in the vows that you exchange with one other. As God looks down upon those exchange of promises He sees something of great beauty. It is a form of godliness. I then refer them to Hebrews 13:5 where Jesus says to us, **"I will never desert you, nor will I ever forsake you."** The grammar of the New Testament Greek presents us a very strong negative statement. The Lord is telling us that He will never, ever desert us, nor will He ever, ever forsake us. The context of this promise is very relevant. The first part of Heb. 13:5 reads, **"Make sure that your character** is free from the love of money, being content with what you have; for He Himself has said, 'I will never desert you, nor will I ever forsake you,'" I say, the context is very relevant because some studies have shown that finances or the use of money is perhaps the number one trouble maker in marriage.

When a couple exchange those wedding vows, when they say in effect to each other, "You can count on me, for I will be there for you for as long as we live," that is a beautiful thing in the eyes of God. It is like the promise that Jesus makes to us as recorded in Heb. 13:5.

Sadly, in our day there are too many couples who repeat those wedding vows without really meaning what they say. In the back of their minds they are thinking, "if this doesn't work out, there is a back door to it. I can get out of it." That is like going to the plate in a baseball game with two strikes against you. Then, it is no wonder that they strike out.

A SPIRITUAL PART OF MARRIAGE

For those who are disciples of Jesus Christ there is also the spiritual part to be considered. Concerning the story of Jesus meeting the Samarian woman at the well at Sychar, I find it easy to imagine that Jesus told her and the man she had been living with to get married. And from that point on they found their relationship greatly enriched, not only by the awareness of belonging to one another in the oneness of marriage, but also in their growing awareness of Jesus Christ in their lives.

APPENDIX IV

THE TWENTY-FOUR ELDERS

*Pursuant to our consideration of
Revelation chapter four.*

Commentators have been divided on the interpretation of the twenty-four elders mentioned in Revelation chapter four with regard to two alternatives: men or angels. Some say they must be another class of angels, while others say the number twenty-four is a symbolic number speaking of men and women who have been redeemed and are now worshipping before the throne of God in Heaven. I definitely lean to the latter view.

BY WAY OF CONTRAST

We will now consider the mountain of evidence set forth in Scripture that indicate that the **"four living creatures"** of Revelation chapter four, verse six are indeed a class of angels who are present at the throne of God in Heaven. By way of contrast there seems to be very little evidence that the mention of the twnty-four elders is a reference to still another class of angels.

ISAIAH CHAPTER SIX

In Isaiah chapter six we read of a class of angels referred to as "Seraphim."

> **"In the year of King Uzziah's death I saw the Lord sitting on a throne, lofty and exalted, with the train of His robe filling the temple. Seraphim stood above Him, each having six wings: with two he covered his face, and with two he covered his feet, and with two he flew. And one called out to another and said, 'Holy, Holy, Holy, is the LORD of hosts, The whole earth is full of His glory (Isa. 6:1-3)."**

Comparing this class of angels with the "four living creatures" of Rev. chapter 4 we note that they are connected by the reference to the presence of God in the temple and that they have six wings. The beings in Rev. 4 are connected with the throne of God in heaven and they also have six wings. This would seem to suggest that they are like or are the Seraphim of Isaiah 6 and that they also are angels.

Furthermore, there is the reference in Revelation chapter four and in Isaiah chapter six to the holiness of God. "And they cried out to one another, **'Holy, Holy, Holy, is the Lord of** hosts, The whole earth is full of His glory (Isa. 6:3).'" And in Rev. 4:8 we read, **"HOLY, HOLY, HOLY, *IS* THE LORD GOD, THE ALMIGHTY, WHO WAS AND WHO IS, AND WHO IS TO COME."**

It is safe to say then, that the four living beings in Revelation chapter four are Seraphim.

EZEKIEL CHAPTERS ONE AND TEN

Even more compelling is the record of a class of beings found in Ezekiel chapters one and ten who are called "Cherubim." We read;

> **"As I looked, behold a storm wind was coming from the north, a great cloud with fire flashing forth continually and bright light around it, and in its midst something like glowing metal in the midst of the fire. Within it were figures resembling four living beings; And this was their appearance: They had human form. Each of them had four faces and four wings. ...And the form of their faces, each had the face of a man; all four had the face of a lion on the right and the face of a bull on the left, and all four had the face of an eagle (Ezekiel 1:4,5,6,10)."**

Looking again at Rev. chapter four we read concerning the four living creatures, "**The first creature was like a lion, and the second creature like a calf, and the third creature had a face like that of a man, and the fourth creature was like a flying eagle. And the four living creatures, each one of them having six wings, are full of eyes around and within; and day and night they do not cease to say, 'HOLY, HOLY, HOLY is the LORD GOD, THE ALMIGHTY WHO WAS AND WHO IS AND WHO IS TO COME (Rev. 4:7-8)."**

In these verses we see a connection to the Seraphim of Isaiah six who have six wings and cry out, "Holy, Holy, Holy," while the four faces mentioned here connect us to the four faces of Ezekiel chapter one. We note that in Ezekiel 10:1 and throughout chapter ten of Ezekiel they are called Cherubim. Of great significance is the description of God's throne and the One who sat on it which is found in Ezekiel chapter one:

> **"Now above the expanse that was over their heads there was something resembling a throne, like lapis lazuli in appearance; and on that which resembled a throne, high up, was a figure with the appearance of a man. Then I noticed from the appearance of His loins and upward something like glowing metal that looked like fire all around within it, and from the appearances of His loins and downward I saw something like fire; and *there* was a**

radiance around Him. As the appearance of the rainbow in the clouds on a rainy day, so was the appearance of the surrounding radiance. Such was the appearance of the likeness of the glory of the Lord. And when I saw it, I fell on my face and heard a voice speaking.(Ezek.I"26-28)."

This great passage connects well with the description of the throne scene found in Revelation 4:3, **"And He who was sitting was like a jasper stone and a sardius in appearance; and *there* was a rainbow around the throne, like an emerald in appearance."**

Let me sum up this section by noting that Ezekiel 1 and 10, Isaiah 6 and Rev. 4 connect in a number of ways suggesting that the four living creatures of Rev. 4:7.8 are very much like Cherubim and Seraphim. They are a similar class of angels and like the Seraphim and Cherubim they are very much connected in worship and service at the throne of God. Worthy of further study is Revelation chapter 4:7 where we have described the four faces of these living beings: that of a lion, a man, a calf, (some versions use the word "ox" for this created being.) and an eagle. It is interesting that in Ezekiel 10:14 the word for this being is "cherub." I take this to mean that the Cherubim are servants, as is the ox. Many commentators believe that the four faces represent Christ in His four capacities as King, Servant, Man, and Son of God, the eagle seen as a Heavenly being. That which we have in Revelation 4:7 corresponds with a similar description found in Ezekiel 1:10. This would seem to be something of a logo representing the second person of the trinity. Consider also the four-fold portrait of, Christ as presented in the Gospels. In Matthew He is the King. In Mark He is the servant as represented by the ox or bull. In Luke He is the Son of Man while in John He is the Son of God. All of this I suggest to the reader for further study. There a large and very interesting body of truth to be considered with regard to the four living beings who are seen in these passages as connected to the throne of God.

In conclusion I say again that there is a mountain of evidence in support of the thought that the four living creatures of Revelation four are angels. By way of contrast, I see a notable lack of evidence that the twenty-four elders are angels. Where is the body of truth that would indicate that the twenty-four elders of Revelation 4:4 are angels? I don't see It.

CONTEXT, CONTEXT, CONTEXT

In the Real Estate business, it is said that the important thing is Location, Location, Location. In the matter of hermeneutics, or principles of Bible study, of great importance is the consideration of context. It's Context, Context, Context. In verse 4 of Revelation chapter 4 the elders are said to be clothed in **"white garments"** and **"golden crowns"** are on their heads. We don't have to go very far back in the book of Revelation to find similar wording.

In Rev. 3:4-5 we read, "**But, you have a few people in Sardis who have not soiled their garments, and they will walk with Me in white, for they are worthy. He who overcomes will thus be clothed in white garments; and I will not erase his name from the book of life, and I will confess his name before My Father and before His angels.**" We see this promise fulfilled in the throne scene of Rev. 4. They are seen before the throne of God, dressed in white, signifying that they have been true to the Lord, even in the trials of life.

If we go back one more chapter in Revelation, back to chapter 2, verse 10 we find a reference to a special crown. We read, "**Do not fear what you are about to suffer. Behold the devil is about to cast some of you into prison, so that you may be tested, and you will have tribulation ten days. Be faithful unto death, and I will give you the crown of life (Rev. 2:10.**" This crown is mentioned in the book of James, verse 12 of chapter one, "**Blessed is the man who perseveres under trial; for once he has been approved, he will receive the crown of life which the Lord has promised to those who love Him.**" Needless to say, we are speaking about men and women who follow Christ. We have no reason to see them as angels.

OTHER CROWNS

The apostle Paul writes about crowns in reference to the Greek games. He writes, **"Everyone who competes in the games, exercises self-control in all things. They then *do it* to receive a perishable wreath, but we an imperishable** (I Cor. 10:25)". He writes in II Timothy 2:5, **"Also if anyone competes as an athlete, he does not win the prize unless he competes according to the rules."** In still another passage he refers to a "crown of righteousness," **"...in the future there is laid up for me the crown of righteousness, which the Lord, the righteous judge, will award to me on that day; and not only to me, but also to all who have loved His appearing** (II Peter 4:8)."

As does John in the Rev. 4:4, and as does James in the first chapter of his epistle, verse 12, and as does Paul in the three passages we have mentioned above, so also does the Apostle Peter in I Peter 5:4. In writing about the faithful pastor he writes, **"And when the Chief Shepherd appears, you will receive the unfading crown of glory."** In all of these passages the Greek word is "stephanos."

W.E. Vine in his "Expository Dictionary of New Testament words, page 258 writes, "Stephanos...denotes (a) the victor's crown, the symbol of triumph in the games or some such contest; hence by metonymy, a reward or prize; (b) a token of public honor for distinguished service, military prowess etc., of nuptial joy, or festal gladness.... It was woven as a garland of oak, ivy, parsley, myrtle or olive, or in imitation of these in gold [Vine, page 258]." He notes that in contrast to the garlands of earth, Peter speaks of "**an unfading crown of glory** (I Peter 5:4)."

Vine goes on to say that "in other passages it stands as an emblem of "life, joy, reward and glory…" [W.E. Vine, page 258].

BACK TO REVELATION 4:4

All of this is to say that the 24 elders mentioned in Rev. 4:4 have been rewarded with the emblem of victory, triumph and joy. They have been victorious in what we might call, the game of life, or perhaps the spiritual battles of life. The **"crown of life"** (Rev. 2:10,) celebrates victory over death. "**The crown of righteousness**" (II Tim. 4:8) is emblematic of victory over sin. The crown received with regard to the Greek games means that one has not only won, but also competed according to the rules.

Furthermore, we read in Rev. 4:4 that the 24 elders are seen as sitting on golden thrones. Part of their reward is to somehow share in the reign of Christ. The promise extends to all of those represented by the 24 elders. It should be obvious that we do not have in view angels, but men.

THEY CAST THEIR CROWNS
AT THE FEET OF JESUS

We read in Rev. 4:9-10, **"And when the living creatures give glory and honor and thanks to Him who sits on the** throne, to Him who lives forever and ever, the twenty-four elders, will fall down before Him who sits on the throne, and will worship Him who lives forever and ever, and will cast their crowns before the throne, …"

I believe these redeemed men and women are saying, "No Lord, all the glory belongs to You, not us." Whatever the nature of the rewards for believers will be, all the glory belongs to the Son of God who has redeemed us by His precious blood.

TWENTY- FOUR DIVISIONS OF PRIESTS

There are some commentators who point out that in the Old Testament record Israel's priesthood was divided into twenty-four courses or divisions and that therefore their responsibilities of service would rotate from one to another. We read concerning **"Zacharias, of the division of Abijah; …now it happened *that* while he was performing his priestly service before God in the *appointed* order of his division, according to the custom of the priestly office… (Luke 1:5,8,9)."** It was king David who divided the priesthood into twenty-four courses or divisions. Yes, we read in Rev. 5:10, **"You have made them to be a kingdom and priests to our God; and they will reign upon the earth."**

THE ONE ARGUMENT

This brings us to the one argument presented by some, that the twenty-four elders are a class of angels. This is found in verse 9 and 10 of Rev. 5. **"And they sang a new song, saying, 'Worthy are You to break its seals; for You were slain, and purchased for God with Your blood _men_ from every tribe and tongue and people and nation. You have made them to be a kingdom and priests to our God; and they will reign on the earth."**

The argument is that the words, "men", and "them" and "they" in these two verses seems to suggest that some group other than men are speaking about men. We note that the word "men" is found in italics in our translation, indicating that it is not actually found in the Greek text. But the words "them" and "they" in Rev. 5:10 would seem to support the thought that the word "men" in verse nine is a good translation. The point is made by some then, that the twenty-four elders are angels and are referring to the blessing that God has given to men. I find this argument weak in contrast to all that we have said above. Don't we today sometimes refer to men, even though we are men? More importantly, I think that the twenty-four elders are marveling at the fact that our God has sacrificed His Son for the sake of men, such as us, who are so undeserving of such blessing. The twenty-four elders are referring to what God has done for men who are so sinful, and are thinking of themselves as such ungodly and undeserving men.

TWELVE PLUS TWELVE EQUALS TWENTY-FOUR

Again, we come to the matter of context, even though the references are a little more removed in the book of Revelation from chapter four. In Rev. chapter 21 we have the wonderful description of the New Jerusalem. In that chapter we find that the number 12 is found once in reference to the nation Israel and once referring to the church. We read concerning the New Jerusalem:

> **"It had a great and high wall, with twelve gates, and at the gates twelve angels; and names *were* written on them, which are *the names* of the twelve tribes of Israel (Rev. 21:12)."**

> **"And the wall of the city had twelve foundation stones, and on them were the twelve names of the twelve apostles of the Lamb (Rev. 21:14)."**

To me this indicates that we have two classes of people living in the New Jerusalem, the Old Testament saints made up of Jews who were justified by faith, men like Abraham and David (See Romans 4:3-6), and those were saved by faith in the church age and thus were part of the church which has its foundation in the twelve apostles. The simple math of it is twelve plus twelve equals twenty-four. It seems to me that the number 24, when referring to the elders of Revelation chapter four, is a symbolic number referring to God's people of all ages who will someday spend eternity in the New Jerusalem. A parallel passage, I believe, is Hebrews 12:22,23:

"But you have come to Mount Zion and to the city of the living God, the heavenly Jerusalem, and to myriads of angels, and to the general assembly and church of the firstborn who are enrolled in heaven, and to God, the Judge of all, and to the spirits of the righteous made perfect."

In Revelation 4:4 the "twenty-four elders" represent figuratively all of God's people, Old and New Testament saints, and they have been raptured before the arrival of the seven-year period known as the tribulation. They have received their rewards for their faithfulness to Christ. They have cast their crowns at the feet of Jesus and are now looking forward to the days of the "new heaven" and "new earth," when all of God's children will worship Him in the New Jerusalem.

BIBLIOGRAPHY

Alexander, Joseph Addison: Commentary on The Book of Acts, (Grand Rapids, MI, Zondervan Publishing House, reprinted 1956)

Bruce, F.F., Commentary on the Book of Acts, (Grand Rapids, MI., WM. B. Eerdmans Publishing Co. reprinted 1986)

Carter, Charles W. and Earle, Ralph: The Acts of the Apostles, (Grand Rapids MI., Zondervan Publishing House,) reprinted in 1973

Chafer, Lewis Sperry, Systematic Theology, (Victor Books, Scripture Press Pub.) 1983

Humberd, R.T. Commentary on Revelation, 1944, out of print

Linsey, F. Duane, Zechariah, The Bible Knowledge Commentary, Old Testament; editors; John F.Walvoord and Roy Zuck, Wheaton, Il. (Victor Books,) 1985

McCague, Mrs. Floyd, Little Boat Twice Owned, (Living Stories, Publishers) 1966

MacArthur, John, Jr.: The MacArthur New Testament Commentary, Acts 1-12, (Chicago, The Moody Bible Institute, 1994)

McGee, J. Vernon: Acts Chapters 1-14, Thru the Bible Commentary Series, (Nashville, Tennessee, Thomas Nelson Inc. 1975)

Morgan, G. Campbell: The Acts of the Apostles, (New York, Fleming H. Revell Company 1924).

My Glory Magazine, Apples of Gold, (Friends of Israel Ministry, January/February 2021)

New American Standard Bible Dictionary, Kinsman Redeemer, p. 79

New King James Study Bible, (Nashville TN, Thomas Nelson Inc. 1982)

The Moody Handbook of Theology: ed. Paul Enns, (Chicago, The Moody Bible Institute, 1989).

Seiss, J. A. The Apocalypse, (Grand Rapids, Mi. Zondervan Publishing House,)

Thomas, Robert, Revelation 8-22, An Exegetical Commentary, (Chicago, Ill, Moody Press, 1995.)

Unger, Merrill F., Unger's Commentary on The Old Testament, Vol. 1 Genesis through Song of Solomon, (Chicago, Moody Press.)

Vine, W.E., Vine's Expository Dictionary on the Old and New Testaments, (Nashville, Thomas Nelson Publishers, 1977.)

Walvoord, John F., The Revelation of Jesus Christ, (Chicago, Ill, Moody Press, 1966)

Printed in the United States
by Baker & Taylor Publisher Services